I0101918

Political Awareness of Sindhi Community

With Special Reference to Ahmednagar City

Prin. Dr. Bal Kamble

Diamond Publications

Political Awareness of Sindhi Community
Prin. Dr. Bal Kamble

First Edition : September, 2016

ISBN : 978-81-8483-696-7

© **Diamond Publications**

Cover Page
Sham Bhalekar

Typesetting
Sandhya Kamat

Published by
Diamond Publications
264/3 Shaniwar Peth, 302 Anugrah Apartment
Near Omkareshwar Temple, Pune - 411 030
Tel No. 020-24452387, 24466642
info@diamondbookspune.com

Buy online at
www.diamondbookspune.com

Sole Distributor :
Diamond Book Depot
661 Narayan Peth
Appa Balwant Chowk
Pune 411 030
Tel. - 24480677, 66020282

All rights reserved. No part of this book may be reproduced or utilised in any form and by any means, electronic or mechanical, including photocopying, recording or by any information storage or retrieval system, without permission in writing from the publisher.

Dedicated to Hon'ble Dr. Anil Patil Saheb,
the Chairman of Rayat Shikshan Sanstha,
a visionary and active educationalist who is ably
and selflessly propelling the chariot of Rayat Shikshan Snastha
founded by late Padma Bhushan Dr. Karmaveer Bhaurao Patil
for the upliftment of the masses.

Preface

India is ornamented with diversity of various castes, sub-castes, religions, culture, regions, creeds, languages, sects and histories. 'Unity in Diversity' is our nation's characteristic feature. The study of such diversity is nothing but the study of various caste groups in India. The tradition of studying Indian society through castes and groups is seen majorly in social issues in Indian society. The study on the caste groups gained importance due to the new awakening among other backward castes because of the Mandal Commission and incidence of achieving the Independence.

While writing the history of society only the campaigns of kings, their defeats and victories, acquisitions of lands and dates were taken into consideration which gave it a limited form. On the other hand, the real history of that society and the influence of changes happened in social, cultural, political milieus were neglected. While putting the history and political history to be specific, the particular community, its development, its strengths, its weaknesses, its socio – economic, political developments, the mutual relation of such elements with each other and its analysis, dissection and unbiased theorization can result into objective history of that society. In this way, the collection of objective information about smaller castes groups can result into the real picture of the society. Therefore, the book 'The Political Awareness of Sindhi Community' by Dr. Bal Kamble, which puts the picture of the Sindhi Community which settled in India after the partition is seminal for all the social elements.

While accepting the study of Sindhi Community as a thesis, one has to check its history through religious, cultural, economical and political dimensions. Otherwise, the researcher cannot do an objective study of it. To study this community is nothing but the study of widening differences between Hindus and Muslims and the resultant expression of two nations theory and the splitting of the nation into two nations on the basis of religion. For taking the research forward, the Hindus coming from Pakistan and Muslim migrated to Pakistan, the extreme perils during the process of such migration, inclusion of people as refugees, taking all such elements under a serious study and forming a background for it becomes mandatory. Dr. Bal Kamble has done praiseworthy attempt about such elements in this book.

Review of the literature related to the subject is essential for putting its 'thesis'. A huge study has been done on the subjects like Sindhi Community, Partition of India, Two Nation Theory, Partition based on religion, the problems of the refugees, the decisions taken about them and their implementations, the literature regarding all such factors is widely existent in history and literature. 'Partition' is the chief issue in Sindhi Literature and the grief in the partition, its problems, memories, their traditions, festivals are at the core of their literature and it does not cross the circumference of the sad reminiscence of the partition.

A large amount of writing is found about the issues like Hindu-Muslim relations in India, invasions of Muslim rulers on Indian terrain, successive British rule on India, the role of both communities in the Great Mutiny of 1857, the splitting among Hindus and Muslims caused by the Britishers' policy of 'divide and rule' , resultant rise of Muslim League and Hindu Mahasabha, the attempt of Congress of keeping the unity of Indian Society, excessive ambitiousness of leadership of every community, resultant two-nations' theory, the attempts made by constituent assembly, the curse of partition along with the bliss of freedom to the nation, the psychology of refugees, etc. The discussions and letters in constituent assembly are minutely described by Sir Mourice

Gwyer and A. Appadurai in 'Speeches and Documents on the Indian Constitution'. But Sindhi is written in Arabic script hence the writing of Sindhi writers is in Arabic script. In result, the writers and readers in Marathi are ignorant about Sindhi Literature. But when that Literature was translated into Hindi, English and other languages or written in those languages, it got the real acquaintance by all. Most of the detailed information about Sindhi Community is generally received from U.T. Thakur and his book 'Sindhi - Culture', K. R. Malkani's 'The Sindhi Story', 'Sindhi Souvir' by Gangaram Samrat, 'Adam- ai- Adib' by Govind Malhi, 'Language, Literature and society' by Rohida Satish, the huge writing done by Bheromal Maharchand Advani and the time to time published literature by Indian Institute of Sindhology. Along with it a huge contribution is done by Saint Lila Shah , Sadhu T. L. Vaswani, Dada Vaswani and the literati like Dr. Ram Panjwani. Apart from the above mentioned literature and sources, some serials and the movie like 'Tamas' reveal the tragic picture of the process of the partition. Sindh Province was the part of Mumbai (Bombay) Province from 1847 to 1936. The administration of Sindh Province was done from the Mumbai (Bombay) as a capital. Such information is sourced from historical documents.

The Sindhi Community, which came to India as refugee and lived in various cities of India by forming camps and colonies during 1948 and 2016, was Hindu by religion. But the differences of language, customs, social structure and their victimization on the basis of religion gives us enough scope to understand the community's psychology. The Sindhi Community is still able to keep its separate identity despite of coming to India and becoming the part of Indian society. It is necessary to understand its psycho analysis. While understanding the psychology of migrated communities, the resultant 'Changes' create seminal impact on the social psyche. Because change and fear are closely related. Nature has the characteristic of change / transformation. Human being is also adaptative to changes. While doing this, the feeling of 'Fear of loss' and the resultant 'instinct to resist change' arise. The continuously arising changes will result into failure and the attempts will go in vain, it will result into our extinction / annihilation, such feelings related to 'Fear of Failure' keeps the society under anxiety. Apart from these feelings, the transformations related to beliefs and systems also results into constant fear. Human being continuously protects his own beliefs, customs, traditions and values as a social animal. The continuous changes may cause shocks to such elements. Therefore, such a community keeps itself alienated. Here it becomes necessary to think about the resultant Xenophobia and the clashes between refugees and localites, struggles of vested interests or the resultant reaction of fear of loss, etc through anthropological and sociological dimensions. While analyzing a migrated community, it also becomes necessary to study it through Geographical perspectives. Because regional boundaries keep the 'Social Systems' safe. When a community has to lose its own land, it has to face the issue of identity.

From the issue of identity crisis many other sub-issues arise. Among them the issue of Legitimacy, issue of Penetration, issue of Integration, problem of Participation, problem of Distribution are more crucial. Hence, it is important to note the reference of political development and above mentioned elements. The fear of extended opinion arises because of inclusion of the process of political development of any community and its analysis, dissection, and understanding. But again the social elements have to be studied in the light of interdisciplinary attitude in Social Sciences. Dr. Bal Kamble has put the subject of 'Political Awareness of Sindhi Community' within the framework of research with a definite focus. Because a researcher has to focus on certain limited issues with great depth and profundity. Dr. Bal Kamble has put a perfect expression of Ahmednagar city, Sindhi

Community dwelling in the city and its political awakening in his book by following research ethics.

The partition of Hindustan was based on the element of religion. And during the process of partition some Muslims went to newly formed Pakistan and some Hindus came to India. Sindhi – Hindu Community is one community among those Hindus. Muslim Community stayed in the Sindh region while others like Sindhis and Sikhs had to leave their region. They grabbed the properties of Sikhs and Sindhis who had left the Sindh Province. Sikhs, at least could gain their region. But the refugee Sindhis had to leave every aspect of their identity at their native place. They had to leave their motherland, their own region, the place where their forefathers dwelt, and a rich cultural background behind to come to a completely new land. The Hindu Community in India accepted these refugees as Hindus by letting them keep their separate characteristics, language, customs, separate identities, etc. All such information is received from this book. On the other hand, the Muslims went from India receive a subordinated treatment there and are called as 'Mahajor'. But Indian Society very gracefully accommodated refugee communities. I would like to mention this fact intensely.

Some fundamental differences are intensely seen in the Sindhi Community which came to India due to the partition and other caste groups in India. As mentioned above while studying a caste – group in India, the *Varna* system, caste discrimination, graded social structure such quantities are seen in little amount in Sindhi Community. 'Sindhi' is region – based word. Not a caste based word. *Varna* system in India, other castes, backward castes, the awakening of self – consciousness among them after the implementations of the recommendations made by Mandal Commission etc are different from the awakening of self consciousness of Sindhi Community. Because the backward castes and other backward castes were from exploited and neglected class of Indian Society. Contrarily, Sindhi Community had a rich and gracious heritage of the Sindhu River having the wealth of landlords and traders. In the Sindh Province, this community was known for trading. There were four classes among them. First three classes were related to trading and agriculture and the fourth was related to administration. The '*Balut*' system did not exist there but the caste–groups of barbers, washermen and potters did exist there. Jobs and services were as repulsive as dung to them. In result, the proportion of Sindhi people at government service is very less.

Dr. Bal Kamble, while describing the Political Awareness of Sindhi Community talks about the development of consciousness. For this purpose, the process of socialization and from it the process of formation of human being and the process of participation as their aftermath is talked, too. Man is basically a social animal. Therefore, he naturally participates in various social activities and events in different forms and different levels. These events may have social, economical, political or religious forms. At the beginning, when the Sindhi Community was unaware about this land, the feeling was of 'insecurity.' Therefore despite of possessing some 'developed consciousness' this community remained aloof from the local communities. Particularly, it remained alienated from the political process. But after getting established, this community is seen increasingly involved in local, regional and national level political processes. But due to the impressions of feudal system, joint family structure and dominance of traditions and customs, the participation of women is very less as compared to men in all fields.

Though the Sindhi Community has arrived at India as a refugee community, they are attached biologically to the localites because of their Hindu religion. In result, the localites helped them instead of harassing them. The democratic system in India also provided them with appropriate milieu for growth. All these factors led to the involvement of Sindhi

Community in political processes, their socialization and development of consciousness. Consciousness, socialization and participation are complementary to each other and therefore the boundaries among them are not vivid. To analyse through these processes is a difficult task. Such a difficult task is very well done by Dr. Bal Kamble.

There are some characteristics of this community in India. Though they are water worshippers, a kind of religious liberalism is found in them. They believe more in principles like secularism, adherence to work, more trade, small profit, contempt for begging, charity, non-violence and peace. They also believe in customs, traditions. Initially, they had to suffer in adversities but because of their belief in 'work is worship' principle like Protestants, Sindhis have progressed without paining localities. But while gaining economic stability, the political process is neglected. The grief of not having one's own region and the laments of partition were experienced by the first generation. Sindhi is not a provincial language in India. This community could not get the 'minority' status. Absence of reservation, limited population and due to scattered population, they cannot create the pressure of votes.

Initially this community kept itself aloof from political process despite of having rich political heritage. In the later phase, it has maintained its aloofness but by participating in local self - government institutions. The new generation of this community is rapidly changing with the changes in society. Therefore trading outside their camps, participating in social process, to follow the vested interest to be with congress initially then B.J.P. such a journey is done by the community. Sindhi community was mostly involved in solving its own issues during 1948 to 1970. To be stable economically and solve the problems of earning a living were their chief concerns. Their participation in those times was very less. Therefore initially their stance of aloofness was deliberate. By keeping in mind the limitations of this research and the selection of survey method for the research, the conclusion of the research may encounter the limitations. Because the selection of sample, scientific methods for it, available information, and their shortcomings cannot result into any universal theories. For it, one should check one's conclusions and put its suitability and adverseness. Then it becomes more objective and goes closer to scientific supports.

Principal Dr. Bal Kamble has done appraisable venture by working on U.GC. projects on small caste-groups and social studies along with ably handling his duty as a principal. After studying this small community in Ahmednagar city, a good arrangement of fact finding is done by considering the political awareness, participation and socialization of Sindhi Community. This subject can be stretched to many dimensions, as stated above. But the researcher does have his limitations. Within the framework of these limitations, this indeed is a good expression of the topic. Along with this research, by accepting an interdisciplinary attitude, an analysis of Hindu social system, *Varnas* and caste systems in it and the reasons for little value given to them despite of their religion being Hindu and reasons for more development of Sindhi social system, etc. should be studied in future.

With able performance as a principal, Dr. Bal, you are doing research and other ventures, too. This really is worthy of praise. Of course, this only can happen because of your abilities and energy. I personally believe that you have given a substantial contribution as a researcher of Political Science. Be the same attempter in the future too. I bid best wishes to all your future endeavors!

Thank You!

Place : Nashik   **Principal Dr. P. D. Deore**,

Date : 15th September ' 2016   President,

                                     Maharashtra Rajyashastra

                                     and Lokprashasan Parishad

Authors Message

People belonging to various castes and religions reside in Ahmednagar city. Followers of various religions like Hindu, Muslim, Jain, Buddhism, Christian and Sikh live here. Along with them, the people of various castes like Maratha, Marwadi, Mali, Dalit, Sali, Koshti, Koli, Sindhi, Punjabi are also live here. The social, economic, political studies of Jain, Marwadi and Mali communities in Ahmednagar city have been done before. As a researcher and a teacher of Political Science, I also felt the need of such a study about other communities in the city, too. Because the politics, economics and society of particular city cannot be understood merely through the study of one or two communities. It is necessary to concentrate to other communities, too.

As a researcher, I always felt that the Sindhi Community in Ahmednagar City must have done crucial contribution in the political, economical and social spheres of the city. I felt the need to study about the exact situations of the Sindhi Community in Ahmednagar city in the framework of research and therefore I applied for economic assistance to UGC at New Delhi. They provided me with it. I am thankful to them for it. Afterwards I forwarded the final report of the research towards them.

I also felt the need of writing a book on such subject within the framework of research. In result, I could write the book – 'The Political Awareness of Sindhi Community – With Special Reference to Ahmednagar City.'

Principal Dr. Bal Kamble
Rayat Shikshan Sanstha's
Dada Patil Mahavidyalaya, Karjat,
Dist. Ahmednagar.

CONTENTS

1 | INTRODUCTION

Objectives of the Study, Meaning of Political Awareness and Research Methodology

The people of different castes and religions live in Ahmednagar City. The population of Ahmednagar, according to the census report of 2011, is 3,50,859 (Three Lacs Fifty Thousand Eight Hundred Fifty Nine). This population is divided into social groups like the Hindus, Muslims, Non-Marathis, Christians etc. The distribution of religion-wise population in the city is as follows : The Hindus 72.5%, The Muslims 17.5%, The Jain-Marwaris 5.52%, The Buddhists 2.25%, The Christians 3.9% and The Sikhs 0.18%. Alongwith this, the people of different castes like the Marathas, Dalits, Malis, Salis, Koshti, Sindhis, Punjabis etc. live in this city. The research work except the Jain-Marwaris, of any other is not undertaken till date. I think such research work of other communities should be done accordingly. Unless it is done, one can't understand the political, social and economical background the Ahmednagar city with the mere study of one community. Hencefroth, the contribution of other communities in the development of the city is thought about. It has been realized that alongwith the Jain-Marwari community the Sindhi community also contributed vividly in the economical, political and social fields of Ahmednagar city. Therefore, the study of the Sindhi Community is must.

Some important conclusions have been drawn from the study and research of the Jain-Marwari community of Ahmednagar city that resulted in believing that their political participation in the city politics is important. Just to observe the conditions of the Sindhi Community in Ahmednagar city, and to have research in this regards, I have selected this topic for research.

Objectives

1) To study the political awareness of the Sindhi Community
2) To find out the history of Sindhi Community of Ahmednagar.
3) To find out the educational progress of the Sindhi Community as a whole including the study of their migration and trading business.
4) To study the agencies of political socialization of the Sindhi Community.
5) To find out their level of political participation.
6) To find out their interest and activeness in local politics of Ahmednagar.
7) To see their relations with other community people in Ahmednagar i.e. relations with the Maratha, Jain-Marwari, Mali and other castes.
8) To find out their sense of political efficacy.

Meaning of Political Awareness

The concept of political awareness is related to democracy. Therefore, the meaning of this concept can be shown in the framework of democracy. While studying the Sindhi Community is Ahmednagar city and the effect of their political activities on political processes, their results and effects have been considered here. First, the scope of this subject is prefixed. While observing the meaning of political awareness the following points have been taken into consideration.

1) People should actively and sensibly be participated in political institutions. The political participation means the voluntarily, participation of an individual in political process at different levels. The political participation includes voting, canvassing, to work for the political party, active participation in the political meetings etc. Sometimes, actions affecting the formal decision – making – process is also called the political – participation. The political participation is an important feature of the democracy. It is observed that less people in India do taken part in active participation in direct politics

2) It is not only important to take part in politics but alongwith politics, to create pressure group and use it as per needs is also equally important. Through this method the political interests of the community are safeguarded. This is one of the meaning of political awareness.

3) The confidence of an individual in society to act in a certain way to affect the situation is the political efficacy. The citizens have the strong faith about the awareness of their political efficacy and the effect of their political action in political processes. They too believe in political and social changes through their individual actions. One should note here that to be aware of political efficacy doesn't mean actions. To feel this is the important feature of the Democracy.

4) Politics doesn't mean the political institutions and the pressure group only. But it means "lobbying" for the decision making process to be moulded accordingly and continuously, making lobbying, any community is trying to develop this awareness. The 'lobbying' means to standardize efforts regarding the specific planning and its attitude. The decision making process is affected by allowing professions, trading interests.

5) To organize the community and not to disorganize it, e.g. from get

together of the ladies for the rituals like ' Haldi Kunku' programme to organize the annual gatherings of the community and from it to increase the political mobilization of the community. To organize the progress keeping in mind the customs and traditions of the community. Such formal and informal programmes help the community people, to get ready for the specific political actions. The youth, women, traders, factory owners and such groups should be mentally prepared for the political action by informing them about the political conflicts and their various attitudes about it.

6) The political attitude means individual's preference and liking to express one's thoughts regarding the political situation, events or persons. To observe the people's views regarding their political rights, independence and equality. If these are biased on the side of independence and equality that community declared to be the community of having the political awareness. If these values are unknown to these people, or their attitude is opposite to it, there lacks the political awareness. Obviously, their political awareness remains on the circumferences or on the borders due to traditional attitude and never it occurs at the center of politics.

Research Methodology

This study was based on the field-work research. The population of Sindhi Community in Ahmednagar city is 16070. Out of this some are the industrialists, traders, educationists, social, religious and political leaders. The questionnaire is prepared and in-depth interviews are also conducted for getting important information and data. The following tools are used for the collection of data.

1) Observation Method :-

2) Questionnaire and in-depth Interviews (Sindhi industrialists, traders, social, religious and political leaders, educationists).

3) Documentation and Institutional Data. While studying the history of this Community the documentation is used. The important references are known through documentation. An institutional data gave information about this institutions and their development.

The following points are also considered while studying the research methodology

1) The concept of political awareness is presented here. To understand it, the study of caste system and its economical effects have been considered. The stress has been given in this study on the data of sub castes, their internal co-relations, caste organizations etc.

2) The Sindhi Community living in Ahmednagar is not established; but it is displaced. The history of their migration and development is presented here. Their participation in the productions of Maharashtra, also their social, political educational and cultural contribution is considered. To collect this information the questionnaire has been prepared and is filled in up by the Sindhi women, students, traders, political, social religious leaders and businessmen. Also the interview of the political leaders of Sindhi community, educationalists, social and religious leaders eminent personalities in the trades and businesses, youth and women of the Sindhi Community have been organized. This is how the data has been collected to present the history of the Sindhi Community.

3) The political and social moves of Ahmednagar situated Sindhi Community takes place at the city level of Ahmednagar ; especially at the Ahmednagar Municipal Corporation level. The stress has been given on the participation of Sindhi Community in the political institutions and local government. For this, the study of the documents of Election Commission related to Ahmednagar Municipal Council and Ahmednagar Municipal Corporation is studied.

4) Apart from the local politics, does the Sindhi Community of Ahmednagar participate in the elections of Vidhansabha and Loksabha? If so, what is the participation ? To know this the website : www.eci.govt.in of the Election Commission was used.

5) It is also studied, how this community works as a pressure group to protect their interests at informal institutional level. The politics regarding the Credit Societies, Banks etc is controlled by the Sindhi organizations and economical institutions. For this the detailed information of these organizations and institutions have been collected through the observation method. The questionnaire method is also used to collect individual's actions, opinions, attitudes etc. One hundred questionnaires have been got filled in from the social and political leaders, traders, educationists, industrialists, youth and women Sindhis. It became easy to explain the information and statistical data with the help of the information collected through the questionnaire. The interviews of the Sindhi stalwarts from different fields are also collected. This helped a lot while studying the Sindhi community in details.

2 | A PROFILE OF AHMEDNAGAR DISTRICT AND CITY

Geography

The Ahmednagar District lying between $18^{0}2'$ and $19^{0}9'$ north latitude and $73^{0}9'$ and $75^{0}5'$ east longitudes is situated partly in upper Godawari basin and partly in Bhima basin. The Ahmednagar District is very irregular in the context of map but compact in shape somewhat resembling a slanting cross with a length of 210 kms and a breadth of 200 kms. It has a total area of 17,035 sq. kms. and a population of 45,43,159 (in 2011). The Ahmednagar District is the largest district in the State of Maharashtra in respect of area, occupying some what a central position in the state. According to the 2001 census, the population of Ahmednagar City was 3,50,859.

There are 14 Talukas in Ahmednagar District. They are – Akole, Sangamner, Kopargaon, Rahata, Shrirampur, Rahuri, Parner, Newasa, Shevgaon, Pathardi, Karjat, Shrigonda, Jamkhed and Ahmednagar.

The district is bounded on the north by lgatpuri, Sinnar and Yeola talukas of Nasik district. On the north-east by Vaijapur, Gangapur and Paithan talukas of Aurangabad district. On the east by Georai, Beed, Ashti talukas of Beed district and Bhum and Paranda talukas of

Osmanabad district. On the south by Karmala taluka of Solapur district and on the south-west by Murbad and Shahapur talukas of Thane district.

i) Mountains, Hills and Rivers

The Sahyadari forms a distance of about 60 kms. It also forms a continuous natural boundary between Ahmednagar and Thane district. The highest mountain peak of Maharashtra - Kalsubai is in Akole taluka. The Baleshwar and Harischandragad mountain ranges are in the district.

There are many rivers which flow through Ahmednagar district. They are Godavari, Pravara, Bhima, Mula, Sina, Adula, Mahalungi and Ghod.

ii) Geology

The systematic geological mapping of Ahmednagar District has not yet been taken up by the Department of Geological Survey of India. The information is available only through the reports submitted by the officers of Geological Survey of India. The geological structure says no minerals of economic importance are available in the Ahmednagar district.

iii) Climate (rainfall, temperature, humidity, cloudiness and winds)

The climate of Ahmednagar district is characterized as a hot summer and general dryness during major parts of the day except during south-west monsoon season. The winter season commences in Ahmednagar district from December and ends in the month of February.

Rainfall

The records of rainfall in the district are available from 13 rainguage stations formed during the period 1947 to 1983. The average annual rainfall in the district is 578.8 mm (22.79"). The Ahmednagar district is known as rain shadow to the east of western Ghats.

Temperature

A meteorological observatory was formed in Ahmednagar in 1891 which is not functioning at present. The cold starts from the midth of November and continues till the end of the February. December is the coldest month in the year, with the average daily maximum temperature of 28.5^{0}C and the minimum 11.7^{0}C. Month of May is the hottest of the year, with the maximum temperature of 38.9^{0}C. The highest maximum temperature recorded at Ahmednagar was 43.7^{0}C on 9.5.1960 and the minimum 2.2^{0}C on 7.1.1945.

Humidity

In Ahmednagar district, the air is generally dry from the February to May and particularly so in the afternoon when the humidity is about 20 percent on an average.

Cloudiness

In Ahmednagar district, the sky is heavily clouded to overcast, especially during the monsoon season. In the past monsoon period the cloudiness decreases. In rest of the year the sky is clear or slightly clouded.

Winds

Winds are generally moderate with some strengthening in the south-west monsoon season.

iv) Population

The population of Ahmednagar district is 45,43,159. The entire population is spread over 14 talukas of district, out of 45,43,159 population 3,50,859 in Ahmednagar.

Density of Population

The density of population in Ahmednagar district is 239 persons per square kilometer. At every census since 1901 the density of population in Ahmednagar district has been lower than that of Maharashtra. It was natural as the Ahmednagar district is situated in the zone of most unreliable rainfall.

Sex-ratio

Since 1901, the sex ratio of the population of the Ahmednagar district varied between 956 and 1005 while that of Maharashtra between 930 and 958. The sex ratio of Ahmednagar city was 961 in 2011. The sex ration of Ahmednagar district was 939 in 2011.

Caste and Religion

The Hindus are often referred to as a single community but in fact Hindus are found divided into many differentiated groups, which are known as castes. Among the castes, there are a number of sub-castes. The following types of castes are found in Ahmednagar district i.e. Brahmins, Marathas, Marwadis, Salis, Mails etc.

v) Historical Background

'AHMEDNAGAR' the 520 year old historical city in Deccan, is surrounded by ranges of Sahyadri mountain from all the sides.

Ahmednagar is home of Saints and Literatures similarly it is a ground of Hussein Nizam Shah, Sultana Chand Bibi-the great heroine of Deccan and Shahaji father of Shivaji.

The city founded by Ahmed Nizam Shah on May 28, 1490 is said to have rivalled Baghdad and Cairo in splendor. The city was moderate in size and surrounded by walls built of stone and mud. There were 11 gatesset in the circular wall. Today only two gates- the Delhi gate and the Maliwada gate remain.

The period of Ahmednagar Nizamshahi is for about 150 years from 1490 to 1633. It is in this period that Nizam Shahas built beautiful palaces and mosques in and around the city. The architecture of all these palacious buildings and mosques show influence of Indo Islamic and Persian or Turkish architecture.

It was one of the Deccan sultanates, which lasted until its conquest by Mughal emperor Shah Jahan in 1636. Aurangzeb, the last great Mughal emperor, who spent the latter years of his reign. 1681-1707, in the Deccan, died at Khuldabad near Aurangabad in 1707, and a small monument marks the site. In 1759 the Peshwa of the Marathas obtained possession of the place by bribing the Muslim commander, and in 1790 it was ceded by the Peshwa to the Maratha chief Daulat Rao Sindhia.

Ahmednagar was invaded by a British force under General Wellesley and captured. It was afterwards restored to the Marathas, but again came into the possession of the British in 1817, according to the terms of the Treaty of Poona.

Ahmednagar is home to the Indian Armoured Corps Center and School (ACC & S), the Mechanised Infantry Regiment Center (MIRC), the Vehicle Research and Development Establishment (VRDE) and the Controllerate of Quality Assurance Vehicles (CQAV). Training and recruitment for the Indian Armoured Corps takes place at the ACC & S. Formerly, the city was the Indian base of the British Army's Royal Tank Corps, amongst other units. Currently the town houses the second-largest display of military tanks in the world. The exhibit is open to the public.

Some important monuments that are mute witnesses of the Nizamshahi of Ahmednagar are :

Ahmednagar Fort

The Ahmednagar Fort is the main historical monument of the city. The fort was built in 1490 by Ahmed Nizam Shaha to commemorate his victory over Jahangir Khan. The fort was captured by different rulers from time to time and, on August 12, 1803 captured by General Wellsely.

Between 1803 to 1817 many Maratha nobleman and during the Quit India Movement (1942) many Indian leaders were detained in this fort. Jawahrlal Nehru, Sardar Patel and Maulana Azad were confined in this fort from 1942 to 1944. During the period of confinement Pandit Jawaharlal Nehru wrote " The Discovery of India".

Baghrauza

Bagh Rauza or the garden of the shrine where King Ahmed Nizam Shaha is burried, is another important historical monument in Ahmednagar. It is just outside the city on the west side. This is the one of the finest buildings of Ahmednagar styled on the Persian architecture.

Farah Bagh

This palace is about 3 kms southeast of the city. It was built by Niyamatkhan and Chingizkhan for Burhan Nizam Shaha I . Burhan Shah did not like this palace and so it was rebuilt in 1583. This is octagonal palace with flat roof upper storey. Round the palace is a large sized pond which is dry today. Though the palace is in ruins today, it shows four centered ardhes of high dimensions from the side.

Behist Bagh

Behist Bagh Palace is also a neglected historical monument about 5 kms away on the north of the city. This is one of the ruined palaces reminding the golden days of Nizamshah. This octagonal beautiful palace was built in 1506 by Ahmed Nizam Shah and was also surrounded by water and lovely garden in those days.

Damdi Mosque

On the north side of the fort is a stonley structure, notable carvings. This is called Damdi Mosque because the workers who were working at the construction of the Ahmednagar for paid a damadi per day for years and from the amount collected Shahrkhan built this in

1567. The mosque is famous for its arches and decorated minars.

Salbatkhan's Tomb

This historical monument is locally called 'Chandbibi Ka Mahal' and can be seen from any side of the city. It is about 8 kms. away on the eastern side of the city. This also the tomb of Salabat Khan II, the famous minister of Murtuza Nizam Shah I. The tomb is built on a hill called 'Shah Donger' which stands about 3,080 feet above the sea level. The building is octagonal and three storeyed with hugh pointed arches from the tomb one can enjoy a breath taking view of the city and surroundings. It is visible from the distance of many miles because it is a place of interest to the visitors of Ahmednagar city.

Besides these monuments tomb of Shah Sharif (Durgah Diara), Miravali Baba tomb, Kothala Mosque, Rumi Khan's Tomb (Pila Ghumat), Kavi Jung's Mahal, Mangani Mahal, Mecca mosque are important historical monuments of the Ahmednagar city.

vi) Industry

Sugar Industry

Ahmednagar district is known for sugar industry. This is the only district in India, where large number sugar factories are located. Padmashri Shri Vitthalrao Vikhe Patil started first sugar factory at Pravaranagar on the principle of co-operative and became first sugar factory in Asia.

Cotton Industry

Ahmednagar was famous for cotton industries. In Ahmednagar there were two cotton ginning mills. These mills are not present today. Now these two ginning mills are transferred to Keshargulab Mangal Karyalaya and Videocon factory.

Cloth Industry

Ahmednagar is known for cloth industry and trade since ancient times. At present there are nearly 100 cloth stores located at Kapad Bazar. The Sarda Cloth Centre and Kohinoor Cloth Centre are famous in Maharashtra. The powerlooms has taken the place of handlooms in Ahmednagar. The main production on powerlooms are saries and shirts. 'Gundu Sari' is famous for saries and Sarda Fashion Limited (SFL) is famous for readymade shirts.

Industrial Development of Ahmednagar

In 1972, the water problem of Ahmednagar was solved by taking water from Mula Dam. At the same time Mr. Navneethbhai Barshikar, MLA and President of Ahmednagar Municipal Council, Shri P. S. Palande, Collector of Ahmednagar made sincere efforts to start M.I.D.C. (Maharashtra Industrial Development Corporation) at Ahmednagar. Then Government of Maharashtra declared M.I.D.C. at Nagapur, Ahmednagar – Manmad Road. Later on the industrial area was developed at Kedgaon. At the same time Firodiya's Kinetic Engineering Industry was started at Arangaon road. Dhoot Brothers also started Videocon T.V. Factory at Ahmednagar. In Ahmednagar City the Marwadi and Sindhi communities has dominated on industry, trade and service sector.

For last 25 years large and small industries were increased at MIDC. Indian Seamless Metal Tubes, L and T, Kirloskar Bearing Division, Hogonos India, Boots Pharmaceuticals, Chakan Oil Mill, Garware Nylon, Advani Orlycons are some of the famous big industries at Ahmednagar MIDC.

Though an industrial area was started at Ahmednagar still industrial development is not satisfactory. The water scarcity, local politics, trade unions working as pressure groups in industrial development of Ahmednagar.

3 | SINDHI COMMUNITY IN INDIA AND MAHARASHTRA

Sindhis are a socio-ethinic group of the people originating from Sindh, a provice of modern day Pakistan. After 1947, independence of India and Pakistan many Sindhi Hindus migrated to India and settled various parts of our country. Appoximately 6 million Hindus and Sikhs migrated to India while nearly an equal number of Muslims migrated to Pakistan from India. Hindu Sindhis were expected to stay in Sindh following the independence, as there were good relations between Hindu and Muslim Sindhis. At the time of independence there were 1,400,000 Hindu Sindhis, though most were concentrated in cities such as Hyderabad, Karachi, Shikarpur and Sukkur. However, because of insecurity in Pakistan, and most of all, a sudden influx of Muslim refugees from Gujarat, Uttar Pradesh, Bihar, Central Provinces, Hyderabad State, Rajasthan and other parts of India, many Sindhi Hindus decided to leave Pakistan. Problems were further aggravated when incidents of violence broke out in Karachi after independence. According to the census of India 1951, nearly 776,000 Sindhi Hindus migrated to India. Despite this migration of Hindus, a significant Sindhi Hindu population still resides in Pakistan's Sindh province where they numbered around 2.28 million in 1998, while the Sindhi Hindus in India numbered 2.57

million in 2001. The responsibility of rehabilitating refugees was borne by their respective government. Refugee camps were set up for Hindu Sindhis. Many people abandoned their fixed assets and crossed newly formed borders. Many refugees overcame the trauma of poverty, though the loss of a homeland has had a deeper and lasting effect on their Sindhi culture. In 1967 the Government of India recognized the Sindhi language as a fifteenth official language of India in two scripts. In late 2004, the Sindhi diaspora vociferously opposed a Public Interest Litigation in the Supreme Court of India, which asked the Government of India to delete the word "Sindh" from the Indian National Anthem (written by Rabindranath Tagore prior to the independence) on the grounds that it infringed upon the sovereignty of Pakistan.

Resettlement of Refugees

Soon after independence in 1947, a large group of refugees from Sindh in Pakistan, came to India. Adipur was founded by the government of India as a refugee camp. Its management was later passed onto a self-governing body called the Sindhu Resettlement Corporation (SRC). The person credited with the formation of this settlement was Bhai Pratap Dialdas, who requested the land from Mahatma Gandhi for the mostly Sindhi immigrants from Pakistan. 15,000 acres of land was donated by the Maharaj of Kutch, His Highness Maharao Shri Vijayrajji Khengarji Jadeja at the request of Mahatma Gandhi because it was felt that the climate and culture of Kutch resembled that of Sindh. Adipur, like Gandhidham, was built on the donated land to rehabilitate Hindu Sindhi refugees coming from Sindh. The Indian Institute of Sindhology established at Adipur, Gandhidham (Kutch), is a centre for advanced studies and research in fields related to the Sindhi language, literature, art and culture. Ahmedabad's population increased dramatically when many households and individuals of Hindu Sindhi descendants arrived from Pakistan for refuge into Ahmedabad. Kubernagar was established with barracks (houses), which were allocated to the refugees who arrived into Ahmedabad.

The Maharaja of Kutch, His Highness Maharao Shri Vijayrajji Khengarji Jadeja, at the request of Mahatma Gandhi, gave 15,000 acres of land to Bhai Pratap, who founded the Sindhu Resettlement Corporation to rehabilitate Sindhi Hindus uprooted from their motherland. The Shindhi Resettlement Corporation (SRC) was formed with Acharaya Kriplani as chairman and Bhai Pratap Dialdas as managing director. The main objective of the corporation was to assist in the rehousing of displaced persons by the construction of a new town on a site a few miles inland from the location selected by the Government of India for the new port of Kandla on the Gulf of Kachchh. The first plan was prepared by a team of planners headed by Dr. O.H. Koenigsberger, director of the Government of India's division of housing. This plan was subsequently revised by Adams Howard and Greeley company in 1952. The town's foundation stone was laid with the blessings of Mahatma Gandhi, and hence the town was named Gandhidham.

Ulhasnagar, Maharashtra is a municipal town and the headquarters of the Tehsil bearing the same name. It is a railway station on the Mumbai- Pune route of the Central Railway. Ulhasnagar, a colony of Sindhi Hindu refugees, is 61 years old. Situated 58 km from Mumbai, the once-barren land has developed into a town in the Thane district, Maharashtra. Originally, known as Kalyan Military transit camp (or Kalyan Camp), Ulhasnagar was set up especially to accommodate 6,000 soldiers and 30,000 others during World War II. There were 2,126 barracks and about 1,173 housed personnel. The majority of barracks had large central halls with rooms attached to either end. The camp had a deserted look at the end of the war and served as a ready and ideal ground for the independence refugees. Sindhi refugees, in particular, began a new life in Ulhasnagar after the independence in 1947.

Refugee Sindhi Hindus from Hyderabad migrated to Bangalore through Mumbai and Goa. A community housing society was created in Cox Town, with a temple, Shindhi Association and a Sindhi Social Hall, a community hub for celebrations, marriages and festivals such as Holi and Guru Nanak Jayanti. The immigration of the community resulted in the introduction of Sindhi culture and cuisine to the city. Also Sindhi Colony is a major suburb of Secunderabad, India. It was founded to house refugee Hindu Sindhis coming from Sindh, after independence.

Many Sindhi Hindus were dispelled from Sindh after the partition of Indian sub-continent in 1947. These Sindhis departed to the neighbouring Indian state of Gujarat, who were not welcomed there by the local descendant of Hindu communities. Appallingly, these very Sindhi Hindus, partially were accepted as true Hindus, Michel Boivin in his book INTERPRETING THE SINDHI WORLD: ESSAYS ON CULTURE AND HISTORY has described the biased attitude with Sindhi Hindus Jhule Lal, a regional Hindu god who was made the community God of the Hindu Sindhis of India. It played a leading role in the construction of a Sindhi Hindu identity in India.

Sindhi People

The Sindhi people live mainly in the north-western part of India. Sindhis inhabit the states of Rajasthan, Gujarat, Maharashtra and Madhya Pradesh as well as the Indian capital of New Delhi. In India, Sindhi is local language in the Kutchh region of Gujarat. Most Sindhis of India follows the Hindu religion (90%), although Sindhi Sikhs are a prominent minority (5-10%). There are many Sindhis living in various cities in India, including Ulhasnagar, Kalyan, Mumbai, Pune, Ahmednagar, Gandhidham, Surat,Adipur, Gandhinagar, Ahmedabad, Bhavnagar, Bhopal (Bairagarh), Ajmer, Jaisalmer, Kota, Delhi, Chandigarh, Jaipur, Bangalore, Hyderabad, Chennai, Raipur, Indore, Gandia, Nagpur, Jabalpur, Katni, Satna, Sagar, Rewa, Bilaspur etc.

The refugees on reaching the Indian soil were dispersed or accommodated in the numerous relief camps set up by the Directorate General of Evacuation of the Government of India at various centers in Bombay, Kathiawar, Rajasthan and the Central provinces. Refugees arriving by rail at Marwar and Pali were sent to various camps at Rajasthan or to transit camps at Ahmedabad, Ratlam and Khandwa, from where they were again sent to various camps in Bombay. By the middle of March 1948, 12 camps had opened in Kathiawar to accommodate about 32,000 Sindhi refugees arriving in the Kathiawar ports. Similar camps with varying capacities were opened at Bikaner, Kotah, Udaipur, Jodhpur and other towns of Rajasthan.

In the same period Bombay itself was home to 1,29,000 refugees in the various camps which were taken over the Central Government. Five military camps at Kalyan were made available to these refugees with the ultimate plan of developing a Sindhi township. The camps in Bombay spread across seven districts, with a capacity to accommodate 1,50,000 inmates, received the largest number of refugees from Sindh.

The camps were expectedly crammed and the accommodation, rudimentary. Procurement of sufficient quantity of food, arrangement of medical staff and supplies, blankets etc, had to be rushed. But this heavy expenditure could not be borne for a larger period, as it was a serious drain on the state resources. In order to implement the Government's decision to wind up gratuitous relief by 31st October 1949, the relief camps at Deoli with a strength of 12,200 was closed and its inmates were sent for resettlement to Bhopal, while the remaining 200 families were sent to Alwar and Bharatpur for settlement. By the end of August 1949, Bombay in its 25 relief camps had a total of around 2.1 lakhs inmates, out of which 1.55 lakhs were receiving doles. Ulhasnagar developed into a separate township with a population of hundred thousand while Gandhidham in Kutch was developed into another major Sindhi township with Kandla as a developing port.

In Madhya Bharat the Kerara camp was closed in November 1949, with some inmates being sent to Gwalior for being absorbed as labourers in factories while the others were sent to Grid district for settlement. By the end of August 1949 there were 54000 refugees in various parts of Madhya Pradesh, which reduced further to a mere 13,600 by the end of the year. As the year 1949 drew to a close the three camps at Tilda, Mana and Chakrabhatta were transformed into permanent township for the inmates. The state of Rajashtan held 15,000 refugees by the end of 1949, which was a 75% decline from its strength of 60,000 during the month of August the same year. This reduction was due to migration of some refugees to Alwar and Bharatpur districts, some to Bhopal and other parts of the state for settlement while the others went to Kandla and were absorbed as workers in the construction of the township of Gandhidham. In Saurashtra, there were no regular camps with relief being provided to 28,000 persons who sought shelter in the many evacuee houses, Dharmasalas and state buildings.

The programme of gradual retraction of government's relief operations commenced by early August 1949 with a steady decrease in the cash doles resulting in discontinuation of the doles from November, except to unattached women and children, the old and infirm persons. As the year 1949 came to an end, there were only 4,000 refugees with 75% yet receiving government doles. Similarly refugees were dispersed in Vindhya Pradesh and other places by stopping doles which were continued for some more months in small numbers and were gradually discontinued, though many camps continued to offer shelter for those without alternate accommodation.

The most important of the many Sindhi settlements across the country is Ulhasnagar. It lies at a distance of 34 miles away from Bombay and is designed within an area of three thousand acres to accommodate two hundred thousand people. During those early post partition days, majority of the population lived in one room tenements, which housed from a minimum of 6 to maximum of 20 members, making life really tough for one and all. The town largely comprises of refugees who came in from the rural villages of almost every part of Sindh. The Sindhi township of Gandhidham was more of a business hub. The Sindhu Resettlement Corporation Ltd, a Bombay based Joint Stock company Constructed this township on a land measuring 17,500 acres, which was granted to the corporation under a lease for rehabilitation of the displaced persons.

Besides the towns of Ulhasnagar Gandhidham, Kubernagar (Ahmedabad) and Bairagarh (Bhopal) refugee colonies sprang up as extension or small town lets on the outskirts of the big cities, planned by the government, to facilitate absorption of refugees in the economy of big towns. Bairagarh, originally created for prisoners of the Second World War, sheltered Sindhi refugees in its abandoned barracks. The other township of Kubernagar was designed to house a population of 30,000 and was built near the airfield at a distance of about 4-5 miles away from the city of Ahmedabad within the view of bringing it within the municipal limits of the Ahmedabad Corporation. Ahmedabad supported 41,675 in 1951 with many being absorbed or involved in cloth business in the cloth – producing centre.

A large number of Sindhi refugees have rehabilitated themselves. There was a huge distinction between the economic positions of Muslims who migrated from India and the Sindhis, as bulk of the Urban Muslims who migrated belonged to the lower middle class. Consequently the Sindhis could not fill in the abandoned economy of the Muslims, but by enterprise and hard work they captured local markets in cloth, provisions and sundry goods everywhere. There is a very popular and widespread testimony that Sindh refugees in general are very hard working people.

It is imbibe in their mannerisms that they would never accept defeat and despite circumstances always emerged in flying colours. Despite having to face many unforeseeable circumstances in the new country they never lost hope. Such intent and determination speaks volumes of them being labeled as a community driven by the hunger for success.

Sindhi Festivals

One of the oldest civilizations of human history, Sindhis have a rich and clearly distinct cultural heritage and are very festive. Their most important festival is Cheti Chand, the birthday of Lord Jhulelal. Besides this, they celebrate Akhandi (Akshaya Tritiya) and Teejri (Teej)

Official Status of the Sindhi Language

Although Sindhi was not a regional language in a well- defined area, there were persistent demands from the Sindhi- speaking people for the inclusion of Sindhi language in the Eighth Schedule of the Constitution. The Commissioner for Linguistic Minorities also recommended the inclusion. On 4 November 1966, it was announced that the Government had decided to include the Sindhi language in the Eighth Schedule of the Indian Constitution.

4 | HISTORY OF THE SINDHI COMMUNITY IN AHMEDNAGAR

90% Hindu – Sindhi's migrated to India form the Sindh province of Pakistan after the partition of Hindustan in 1947 [1]. 10% of the Hindu – Sindhi Community lives in Pakistan even today. The Hindu – Punjabi community also migrated to India from the Punjab province of Pakistan along with the Hindu – Sindhi Community. There after the Sindhi Community has been scattered all over India. The community has been settled in Mumbai, Kalyan, Ulhasnagar, Pimpari, Deolali Camp (Nasik), Jalgaon, Pachora, Chalisgaon, Malegaon, Solapur, Nanded, Ahmednagar etc. cities of Maharashtra. Although considered as the refugees [2], the people of this community are settled in all the constituent states in India, now.

Initially, the people of the Sindhi Community were allotted small houses and barracks to reside by the Government in one part of the city. Even rations too were provided by the Government. Later, in the course of time, the people of this community purchased the allotted sites, houses and barracks. Numerous Sindhi colonies have come up in many cities in Maharashtra, today. The Sindhi Community in the city of Ahmednagar, resides at the Sindhi Colony, Tarakpur [3].

The people of the first generation of the Sindhi community toiled hard after their migration to India. They sold clothes on the city footpath; sold pepper mints and biscuits in the train and opened up tea – stalls [4]. In short, the community started the business, smaller in scale and operated through stalls. Later, in the course of time, they succeeded in their business, thanks to their industrious nature. Gaining stability in their business and (Small scale) industry, the philanthropic persons of the Sindhi Community and some institutions founded schools, colleges and built temples and inns for the pilgrims (Dharmashalas)[5].

The Sindhi Community in Ahmednagar

The population of the Sindhi Community in Ahmednagar City is 16,070 [6]. At present this community is settled in a Sindhi colony at Tarakpur, a part of Ahmednagar city. The community resides at one place in the city. It is not because it feels insecure. The real reason is because the Government has allotted the same piece of land for the community. People of the community bought plots as per their economic position. And the community thus has firstly settled at this specific place. This aspect of significant factor related to the observational study of the Sindhi Community will be focussed later in this research.

Majority of the Sindhi Community resides in the Sindhi colony only. The people of the Community have their houses in different part of the city, now. Their jobs and business don't seem to be concentrated at the Sindhi colony alone. In fact different shops owned and run by the Sindhi merchants are now seen at different places of the city, such as the commercial complex owned by the Corporation Sarjepura, G.P.O Road, Chitale Road, Neta Subhash Chowk, Telikhunt, Savedi etc. These are mostly clothes, electronics, electrical items, automobiles, furniture, watch makers, telecom and mobiles, General and departmental goods and grocery shops. The Sindhi business Community has earned a reputation in Hotel business. The past ten years have witnessed the upsurge of the Sindhi businessmen in field of Lottery business[7]. As regards the ' production industry' in the city, the Sindhi community has substantial contribution in Foundry and Ice-cream business.[8]

As regards the financial matters the city, the Marwari and Jain communities seem for have upper hand ; the Sindhi community follows them 99% of the total Sindhi population seems to have settled in the trade of the city. 20% of the women in Sindhi Community are involved in their house hold business. Besides sewing these women prepare papads, wafers, pickles and 'Tikki'. They sell these eatables, same other women of this Community run standard beauty parlours in the city.[9]

Sindhi Credit Society is reputed for its substantial work. Mr. Lalusheth Madhyan, President of the Credit Society and Mr. C. L. Madhyan, Director of the Society emphasized the need for the establishment of such a society. People from the other communities in the city too are the beneficiaries of this Credit Society.[10]

After the establishment of Municipal Corporation (2003) the merchants of the Sindhi Community agitated against the octroi from time to time. Mr. Lalusheth Madhayan is the leader of the agitation. In his studied speeches he pointed out the fear regarding the set back likely to be faced by the city trade after the launching of the octroi.[11]

The Community is also involved in the social cause of the city. It becomes evident especially after the formation of the Sindhi Social Sanstha, how the community participated in the societal activities through their contribution. Equally, the community has been involved earlier in the politics of the Municipal election and later in the Municipal Corporation election. The Sindhi electorates have shown their strength in the local politics by getting their own Municipal candidates purposefully elected.

But, after the involvement of different political parties in the local politics, the Sindhi Community electorates formal themselves divided among various political parties. It is how the candidates of the Sindhi Community suffered defeat at two places in the Municipal Corporation elections of 2003.[12]

The Sindhi Community in Ahmednagar is known for tolerance. It maintains cordial relationship with the other societies. These people also are known for their pleasing conduct.[13] They could comfortably settled themselves in business. The Community is watchful regarding its rights. But according to the intellectuals of this Community, the people of this Community do not demand and favour from the Government as a Community belonging to linguistically minority position. The Sindhi Community should be given the minority status. But this Community will neither agitate nor will it take out morchas to pressurise the favours granted by the government for the minority. This is the view of some of the experts of the Community.[14] The Sindhi Community at Ahmednagar has not asked for any concessions for the Government regarding the issue.[15] But when the Sindhi Community sensed in 2005 that the word ' Sindh' was thought to be dropped from the text of the National Anthem, it suddenly became alert. It was then that the various Sindhi societies got together, took out morchas and agitated constitutionally and brought the strength of their tolerance and solidarity to the notice of the people of Ahmednagar. Various organizations of the Community at Ahmednagar, in the field of education Literature and General Panchayat (body of arbitrators) Sindhi colony panchayat, Sindhi Social Sanstha, Sindhi Nagari Pat Sanstha (Credit Society), Sindhi Yuva Sangh (Youth Organization), Gurukripa Trust etc. submitted the statement to the Government. In their representation they insisted that while composing the National Anthem before the partition the poet, Late Rabindranath Tagore had used the, word 'Sindhi' not denoting as a ' province'. But connoting as the ancient Sindh civilization may also pointed out that the word Sindh reflects the river Sindhu. Realizing the seriousness of the issue the following members of the Sindhi Community, did timely agitation : Lalusheth Madhyan, Daulatram Balani, Damodar Batheja, Kisan Panjawani, Harumal Hiranandani, Bansi Aasnani, Anand Krishnani, Shrichand Sachdev, Jaykumar Khubchandani, Thakur Navalani, Damodar Batheja, C. L. Madhayan, Shrichand Talreja, Jayram Gabara, Sherasheth Kukareja, Purushottam Kukareja, Harijitsing Vadhawa, Anil Sablok etc.[16]

Temples

Situated at Tarakpur in Ahmednagar city, is the temple of Zulelal. Another Zulelal temple a private one, also known as Lal Sanee Mandir at Shree Darda's Bungalows on Gulmohar Road.

The whole Sindhi Community worships Zulelal, the God Varun. The same is considered as them God patron as well. The festival, scheduled before the Ganpati festival and known as 'Chaliho Utsav' is celebrated on grand scale. The entire Sindhi Community worships the God, Zulelal devotedly.

As in the Hindu religion the people of this Community worship the goods and goddesses. They worship the Goddesses on a grand scale. They worship goddess Vaishnavi Devi also. They are also worshipped Lord Vishnu, Shankara, Krishana, Ram, Hanuman and the Sindhi Saints.

A religious ceremony known as Chetichand, falling on the second day of 'Gudhi Padva' is organized by the Sindhi Colony Panchayat. The entire Sindhi Community remain present for this ceremony. Various competitions for students and women folks are held on the occasion. Blood examination, blood pressure etc. health related programmes are conducted by the Sindhi Yuva Manch.[17]

Religious inns for the pilgrims (Dharma Shala)

Same generous and philanthropic Sindhi members of the Community with their own money and also with the money collected by public funds built 'inns for the pilgrims' popularly known as 'dharamshala'. There is one 'dharamshala', Radhakishan Madhyan Dharmashala at Tarakpur. There also is a Bhojwani Hall (Mangal Karyalaya : a wedding Hall) at Maliwada. The well-furnished. Sindhu Mangal Krayalaya (A wedding Hall) at Bhutkarwadi is a multipurpose complex. It caters to various religions, cultural, educational and social functions of the Community. These offices are also made available for the other religions functions of the other communities.[18]

The Sindhi Saints

The Sindhi Saints have a very respectable place in the development of the Sindhi Community. The great work and teachings of Sadguru Swami Sarvandand Maharaj, Shatiprakash Maharaj, Haridasram Maharaj, Jeevan yukta Maharaj and Bhagat Prakashjee Maharaj have been greatly inspiring and enlightening for the entire Community. The birth centenary programme of Shantiprakash Maharaj was celebrated in Ahmednagar in 2007 at Swami Tahuram Mandir on a grand scale.[19] Besides, the birth centenary of the Rastra Sant Godhadiwale Baba (Jalgaon) alias Baba Hardasram was celebrated with religious fervor and delight at 'Sant Godhadiwale Dham' in 2005 [20].

Innumerable Hindu – Sindhis migrated to India after the partition. It was then that the Sindhi Community experience a great solace in form of the Sindhi saints and their philosophy teaching.[21] If the Sindhi saints exemplified the service to all the living creatures they also kept the spiritual torch burning. Many rest house (dhams) and service – centres were opened at many places in India, inspired by the work of the saints. These selflessly striving human service centres are rightly can to be regarded as the glory of the Sindhi Community feeding the Langars' (food served everyday to the devotees). Oldpeople's house, widow-house, cow-house, collective marriage ceremony, informed get together of the prospective bride-grooms, collective thread – ceremony, financial assistance to the poor and the needy, Health Camps (Diagnosis) and cultural programme run and mounded honest by the Sindhi community, one does experience the honest attitude of the community for the social service. [22]

Sects (Panth)

There are about 10 to 12 sects existing in Ahmednagar city. The Sindhi Community in the city, is divided among various sects. Members of other communities also visit the programmes of these sects. The major participation of such programmes, however, remains that of the Sindhi Community. These days the people of Sindhi Community follow there sects whose philosophy of devotion they cherish.[23] Following are the various sets that exist at present in Ahmednagar. Nirankari Panth, Radhaswami Panth, Anandpuri Panth, Asaram Bapu Panth, Dadalaxmi Panth, Shanti Prakash Panth, Prajapati Brahma Kumari (Mount Abu) Panth, Guru Nanak Panth, Sadhu Vaswani Panth and Lilashah Panth.[24]

Nirankarni, Radhaswami and Anandpuri Panths have Punjabi Gurus (Master). These sects in Ahmednagar enjoy a great number of Sindhi Community. There are some Sindhi citizens in Ahmednagar, who belong to the other sects or Panths. The Sindhi citizens that follow Sadhu Vasvani and Lilashah Panth in the city are very few in number.

Various programmes of the sects are held throughout the year. Emphasis is given on Chief programmes like ' Satsang' and Keertan'. A great number of Sindhi citizens remain present for 'Satsang' and 'Keertan' of various sects on every Wednesday and Sunday. [25]

Gurunanak Panth had a great influence on the Community some

years back, so tell the senior people of the city. The Sindhi members, however, are not found in good number in these sects. The influence of these sects on the Punjabi society in the city is still great even to-day. 'Tikanu' (known as Tehuram Mandir) are only at Maliwada, Bhutkarwadi and Tarakpur, in the city to-day.[26] Less number of people in the Sindhi Community visit them. The creation of various sects (Panth) and the division the Sindhi Community seem to be only reason for the poor number. [27]

Castes and Sub-Castes

The Sindhi Community is free from caste and class difference the view of many experts in the society. Therefore, sub-castes are not found in this community. Some merchants in the Sindhi communities do either the business of silver-gold or that of footwears. But such people cannot be treated as belonging to one caste. People in the communities share and solemnise marriages among themselves. The Sindhi Community doesn't entertain the lower higher status discrimination. The reason is imbedded in their occupation. Since 99% of the people are totally immersed in their occupation they have hardly any time for casteism. [28]

Panchayats working in all the parts of the city come under an apex body Panchayat called the Sindhi General Panchayat. Lalusheth Madhyan is the President of this General Panchayat. The Sindhi Colony and Maliwada Panchayat Executive Bodies come under other Panchyat Executive Bodies. Following members executive here. Damodar Batheja, Amarlal Vadhavani, Shrichant Sachdev, Ramesh Tanwani, Rupchandra Motwani, Manakram Matlai and Vadhudev Kachwani. These associations decide the kind and nature of programmes like Chetichand, Chaliho in consultation with the Sindhi General panchayats and execute them accordingly. [29]

The Sindhi Social Institution

The workers in the Sindhi Community with the yearing for social work, got together and founded the Sindhi Social Institution on 23rd Feb. 2003. [30] Anand Krishnani is the president of this institution. Following members in the Sindhi society are on the executive committee : Suresh Hiranandani, Bhagwandas Motiyani, Peetambar Purvaswani, Thakoordas Navalini, Jayram Gabara,, Mahesh Madhayan, Rana Keertani, Jayram Khoobchandani, Roopchand Motwani, Rajesh Sachdev and Tarachand Popatani. The office of the institution is on Mahatma Gandhi Road. Social work has been the cherished aim of this Institution. [31] The institutions has arranged various kinds of functions so far. Among these were : Informal get together of the prospective bride-grooms, health camps (Diagnosis) camp for all the citizens of Ahmednagar, Blood donation camps, felicitation of the meritorious students in the Sindhi Community. In order to create interest in the Sindhi language, Sindhi dramas, Sindhi cinemas and Sindhi dancing programmes have been presented for the last 4-5 years. These programmes draw large audience especially the yang boys and girls and women. The organizers firmly believe that such programmes become instrumental for the spread of Sindhi Language. [32]

Sindhi Language and Literature

In order to preserve and protect the Sindhi language, the Sindhi Community is seen encouraging various programmes. But if this community's effort seems to occupy the social scenario of the community the dismal fact, on the other hand exposes the bitter reality that there just does not exist any independent Sindhi medium school in Ahmednagar. The Ahmednagar Municipal Council founded the first Sindhi school in 1948. Thanks to this school, number of migrated students from the Sindhi Community could avail of the primary education.

Later in the course of time a Sindhi middle school was founded at Sarjepura, Ahmednagar. Number of Sindhi students received their middle school education there. Thereafter a Sindhi High School (from 8th to 11th standard) at Sindhi Colony, Tarakpur, was started. But also an English Medium School was also started in the same building in the afternoon. Eventually, the Sindhi medium school was closed and the parents started sending their wards in English medium school. At present instead of Sindhi medium school, they have Vivekanand English Medium School. The management, the staff and the students belong to the Sindhi Community on large scale. Since the medium of instruction is not the Sindhi mother tongue interest in the Sindhi Language doesn't seem to develop in the new generation, so laments Prof. Lachman Hardwani. The school management, however, is of the view that although the school has English medium, efforts are taken so that students already having Sindhi as second language, may opt it as also optional subject. Since higher education can't be provided in Sindhi Language, parents mostly prefer English medium in school. Because of this fact, view some, the Sindhi students do not seem to be opting Sindhi as a medium of instruction. [33]

'Sindhi Diwas' (Sindhi-Anniversary) has been celebrated every year on 10th April for that 5-6 years in the city, by Sindhi Shiksha (Education) and Sahitya Sanghatana (Literary organization). Sindhi language was given the recognition in 1967 by the Government of India. It is invoked by the institution to speak Sindhi to write Sindhi and to read Sindhi, for the spread of Sindhi Language. [34]

Sindhi Literature

Prof. Lachman Parasram Hardwani, retired Head of the Hindi Dept, Ahmednagar College, has done a great work for the preservation of Sindhi language and literature. His books have been published in

Sindhi, Hindi, and Marathi Languages. His major writing devoted to various lexicons. He has a starpendous contribution in translation : translating Marathi in Sindhi and Hindi, translating Sindhi into Marathi and Hindi into Sindhi. He has also edited a few books. His contribution as a Sindhi Literature is undoubtedly great in Maharashtra and in India. He has penned Marathi – Sindhi and Sindhi-Marathi lexicons. His translations of 'Manchae Shloak, Dnyaneshwari, Tukaram Gatha and Dasbodh in the Devnagari Sindhi script is regarded as an outstanding work. He was awarded the Sahitya Academy Award for translation in 1992. He was also honoured with the Priyadarshani Puraskar in 1996, the Historical Museum Puraskar (2004) and The Nagar-Savedi Puraskar (2006) [35].

Notes and References

1. An Interview with Prof. L. P. Hardwani, educationalist, Ahmednagar.

2. An interviewed with Shri. Jayaram Thadani, Formar Branch Manager, SBI, Krishi Vidhyapeeth Branch, Rahuri. (Dist. Ahmednagar).

3. A discussion with Prof. L. P. Hardwani, educationalist, Ahmednagar on 05/04/2010.

4. An interview with Shri. Jaykumar Khoobchandani, Furniture businessman, Ahmednagar.

5. A discussion with Shri. Harishbhai Khoobchandani, builder, Ahmednagar.

6. Pariwarik Directory of Sindhi Community, Ahmednagar City, Tehuram Mandir Trust, Ahmednagar, 2003.

7. A Discussion with Shri. Govind Talreja, Lottery Dealer, Ahmednagar.

8. A discussion with Shri. Navlani Laxmandas, Sindhi Industrialist, Ahmednagar MIDC on 12/02/2011.

9. A discussion with Shri. Jayakumar Khoobchandani, businessman, Ahmednagar.

10. An Interview with Prof. C. L. Madhyan, Director of Sindhi Credit Society, Ahmednagar on 01/04/2012.

11. News in local newspapers like Samachar, Nava Marahta in May 2004.

12. An Interview with Shri. Damodhar Batheja, Sindhi Political leader, Ahmednagar on 26/12/2012.

13. An Interview with Shri. Thakur Navlani, Sindhi political leader, Ahmednagar.

14. A discussion with Prof. L. P. Hardwani, educationalist, Ahmednagar.

15. A discussion with Mr. Jayaram Thadani, Branch Manager, SBI - Krishi Vidyapeeth, Branch, Rahuri, Dist. Ahmednagar on 07/04/ 2011.

16. News in Pune Sakal (News paper) on the page of 'Maze Nagar' on 03/02/2005.

17. Programme sheet of Chetichand (Gudhi Padua) Anand Mahostva – 2010 held at Ahmednagar.

18. An Interview with Mr. Shankar Andani, Charted Accountant, Ahmednagar.

19. A Phamplet published by Shri. Shrichand Talreja, on behalf of Tehuram Mandir Trust' , Maliwada, Ahmednagar on 06/04/2007.

20. 'Rastra Sant Godhadiwale Baba' an article published in 'Ahmednagar Samachar' by Prof. L. P. Hardwani on 27/03/2005.

21. 'Sindhi Sant Baba Hardas' an article published in Pune Sakal by Shri. Tolaram Raheja, Pimpri, Pune on 02/02/2005.

22. A discussion with Prof. C.L. Madhyan, Charted Accountant, Ahmednagar.
23. An Interview with Mr. Anand Krishani, President, Sindhi Social Institution, Ahmednagar on 14/04/2009.
24. A discussion with Prof. L. P. Hardwani at Ahmednagar on 14/04/2007.
25. A discussion with Prof. L. P. Hardwani and Mr. Jayakumar Khoobchandani at Ahmednagar on 17/04/2007.
26. A discussion with Shrichand Talreja, Trustee of Tehuram Mandir Trust, Maliwada, Ahmednagar on 20/04/2007.
27. A discussion with Prof. L. P. Hardwani at Ahmednagar on 21/04/2007.
28. An interview with Shri. Manohar Gabra, owner of Guru Furniture, Ahmednagar on 01/05/2010.
29. An Interview with Mr. Lalusheth Madhyan, President of Sindhi General Panchayat, Ahmednagar on 30/04/2007.
30. News published in Ahmednagar Nava Maratha (Newspaper) on 24/02/2003.
31. An Interview with Mr. Anand Krishnani, President of Sindhi Social Institution, Ahmednagar on 14/04/2012.
32. A discussion with Mr. Jayakumar Khoobchandani, Businessman and member of Sindhi Social Institution.
33. A discussion with Mr. Jayaram Thadani, Branch Manager, SBI - Krishi Viyapeeth Branch, Rahuri, Dist. Ahmednagar on 22/04/2007.
34. Published News in Sakal and Samachar Newspapers about Sindhi Diwas Programme on 10/04/2007.
35. Published books and Literature of Prof. L. P. Hardwani.

5 | POLITICAL AWARENESS, POLITICAL PARTICIPATION AND POLITICAL SOCIALIZATION OF SINDHI COMMUNITY

Sample of hundred individuals from Sindhi Community of Ahmednagar City has been selected to study their political awareness. This group of one hundred people is a representative group. It has been done to represent the students, political and social leaders, industrialist, professionals (Doctors, Engineers, architectures, Builders, Lawyers etc.) personalities related to education, service sector, trade, women related to service sector and trade, religious leaders and housewives of Sindhi Community. Hence, the selected sample group included all types of people from Sindhi Community. Some of these personalities also have been interviewed.

Alongwith this selected sample group three different age groups represents Sindhi Community – youngsters, middle aged and above fifty. *(See Table No. 5:1)*

5:1   Classification of age groups

Sr. No.	Age group	Quantity	Percentage
0			
2.	35-49	38	38%
3.	Above 50	28	28%
	Total	**100**	**100%**

In short, the selected sample group consists of 34% youngsters between 18-34. The ratio of the youngsters of this Community is co-related with ratio of youngsters from India. Therefore, the attitudes of youth have seen in the sample. In addition to that, the middle age group from 35 to 49 is also observed. The population of this age group is 38%. Therefore aged do get recognition in politics along with the youngsters and middle age group e.g. the political post have been gained after the age of fifty. (L. K. Advani) Hence, the researcher has selected the age group above fifty. As a result, the frame work of Indian politics and the co-related age group have rightly matched with each other in this study. Hence, the researcher got the accurate and proper method of study to work on Sindhi Community of Ahmednagar city and their political awareness, political participation and political socialization.

This study is about the Sindhi Community from Ahmednagar city. Even then this sample group of Ahmednagar city is useful to study and explained the contribution of Sindhi Community in India. So it is not limited to Ahmednagar city only. On the contrary, it is useful to understand complete Sindhi Community in India, regarding their contribution in the field of politics. Therefore, the sample group clearly indicates the political characteristics and political trends in India.

While studying the political awareness, the factor of education has been observed as follows. *(See Table No. 5:2)*

5:2   Educationwise classification of Sindhi Community

Sr. No.	Educational Groups	Quantity	Percentage
1.	Illiterate	05	5%
2.	Primary	17	17%
3.	Secondary and higher secondary	28	28%
4.	Graduation	32	32%
5.	Post Graduation	11	11%
6.	Professional	07	07%
	Total	**100**	**100%**

Above table shows 32% of the people in the Sindhi Community have been founded reached up to the graduation. The follows 28% of the people completed their education up to secondary and higher secondary. 17% of the people have completed their primary education. 11% and 7% of the Sindhi people completed their Post-Graduation and professional education respectively. And the minor percentage of the illiterate people is about 5%.

The following three points are related with politics – Family, responsibility of the family and profession. The responsibility of the family is not but the social binding and profession is related to Community. Therefore, the behaviour in the family and Community may be treated as a political behaviour. *(See Table No. 5:3)*

5:3 Opinions about the family responsibility of Sindhi Community

Sr. No.	Kinds of family responsibility	Quantity	Percentage
1.	House keeping	15	15%
2.	Employment	04	04%
3.	Profession	81	81%
4.	Agriculture	00	00%
	Total	**100**	**100%**

The above table shows that the maximum i.e. 81% of the people are engaged in the professions. Which means 81% of the Sindhi Community people are related with the other community. The employed people are less (4%) in the community.

The research shows that there is a close relationship between the family responsibility and profession. In short, profession is the most important in Sindhi Community. One has to have political behaviour to stabilize the profession because the security in profession is must. The following table shows the nature of professions of Sindhi Community is related to politics. *(See Table No. 5:4)*

5:4 Classification of professions

Sr. No.	Type of profession	Quantity	Percentage
1	Shopkeeping	61	61%
2	Industry	08	08%
3	Employment	04	04%
4	House keeping	15	15%
5	Builder	01	01%
6	Doctor	01	01%
7	Service Sector	06	06%
8	Not responded	04	04%
	Total	**100**	**100%**

The above table shows that 61% of this community people are engaged in shopkeeping. 15% of them in housekeeping 8% of them are factory owners, 4% of them are employees, 6% of them are in service sector and doctors, builders are not more than 1%.

The newspapers play the important role in political socialization of Sindhi Community. 83% of the Sindhi Community people are related to the newspapers. The community believes that the newspaper is an important media to get information about political events, political ups and down and minute details about marketing around. The Sindhi Community do take earlier decision, due to information received regarding the political changes.

The following table shows that Sindhi Community relation with newspapers. *(See Table No. 5:5)*

5:5 Classification of the relation between Sindhi Community and Newspapers

Sr. No.	Media literate and illiterate	Quantity	Percentage
1.	Newspapers readers	83	83%
2.	Non-newspapers readers	17	17%
	Total	**100**	**100%**

Along with the newspaper reading the Sindhi Community watches the programmes on T.V., Therefore, T.V. is one of the important media for the political socialization of Sindhi Community.

The following table shows the relation between the Sindhi Community and watching T.V. *(See Table No. 5:6)*

5:6 T.V. watches and non-watches

Sr. No	T.V.watchers and Non-watchers	Quantity	Percentage
1.	T.V. watchers	100	100%
2.	T.V. non-watchers	00	00%
	Total	**100**	**100%**

The following table shows the relation between the Sindhi Community and using social media. *(See Table No. 5:7)*

5:7 Social Media Users and Non Users

Sr. No.	Social Media Users and Non Users	Quantity	Percentage
1	Social Media Users	90	90%
2	Social Media Non Users	10	10%
	Total	**100**	**100%**

Along with the T.V. watching the Sindhi Community highly using social media tools like Whatsapp, Facebook and Twitter regularly. It is observed that the social media is very much useful for development of trade, business and commerce of Sindhi Community.

The participation of Sindhi Community is also takes place, due to Sindhi Community organizations. Political, social and religious organizations have been observed in Sindhi Community. The religious and social organizations do politicization of Sindhi Community.

The relations of Sindhi Community with religious, social and political organizations are as follows. *(See Table No. 5:8)*

5:8 Relation of Sindhi Community with other organizations

Sr. No	Type of organization	Quantity	Percentage
1.	Religious organization	20	20%
2.	Social organization	75	75%
3.	Political organization	02	02%
4.	Not responded	03	03%
	Total	**100**	**100%**

75% of the people in the Sindhi Community believe in social organization, which clearly indicates the Sindhi Community people believe in socialization. Welfare of the community is always at the prime importance and this has been known as politics. It has been observed that according to Sindhi Community, the socialization and politics are two sides of the same coin. 20% of the Sindhi Community people called their social organizations as religious one, which means, they do keep in contact with community believing in the religious frame work. They do take interest in political moves in the disguise of socialization and religious moves. This obviously shows that the Sindhi Community has no direct relations with the politics but through social and religious organization they know political moves. One may call it, a way of entering the politics through social and religious organizations, which shows their high political socialization.

In the context of Indian politics, it is defined as to withdraw ones community from customs and traditions and cope up it with modernization. This type of politics had been executed by Justice M. G. Ranade, Maharshi V. R. Shinde, Mahatma Phule, Dr. B. R. Ambedkar and Rajarshi Shahu Maharaj. The Sindhi Community also applies the same in the framework of politics and political socialization of the Sindhi Community occurs in the same framework. The Sindhi Community must become modern, which means liberalist. The Sindhi Community must protect its welfareness in this ultra modern framework and for that must leave customs and traditions. The meaning of modernization means the use of newspapers, news channel, public opinion and the organizations of the people. The Sindhi Community does this political change in their community. 78% of the people believed in the change of the Sindhi Community. Only 3% of the people believe in the traditional ways, which clearly indicates the politicization of Sindhi Community in the modern political framework as occurred. *(See Table No. 5:9)*

5:9 Opinions regarding changes in Sindhi Community

Sr. No	Types of changes in Sindhi Community	Quantity	Percentage
1.	Changes in customs and traditions	78	78%
2.	Changes in Modernization	19	19%
3.	Community to remain traditional	03	3%
	Total	**100**	**100%**

The Sindhi is minority community based on linguistic classification but its identity is not minority. And the notable reason for that the Sindhi Community identifies itself with Hindu community. The word Sindhi identities itself with its geographical sphere, where as Sindhi Community openly accepts its identity with majority Indian Hindus. It clearly shows that political socialization of Sindhi Community has occurred in the framework of Hinduism. The Sindhi Community has not cope with on large scale with Muslims and Dalit people. Therefore, the political values and attitudes of Sindhi Community are the Hindu political views and attitudes. It is observed that the Hindu attitudes have greatly affected the political socialization of the Sindhi Community. This point clearly indicates the relation of Sindhi Community with other community. *(See Table No. 5:10)*

5:10   Relations between Sindhi and other communities

Sr. No.	Relations with different communities	Quantity	Percentage
1.	Hindus	73	73%
2.	Muslims	05	05%
4.	Remaining others (with Christians and Nav Buddha)	22	22%
	Total	**100**	**100%**

The above table clearly indicates the maximum relation of Sindhi with Hindus. At the same time their relations with Christians and Nav Buddhas are also good, but the number of Christians and Nav Buddhas in relation with Sindhi is less. In Ahmednagar large number of Christians live near Sindhi colony. It proved helpful to Sindhi Community for commercial purpose. In short, Sindhi Community is modern. But it does not appear that on social and religious level. Sindhi Community is different from Hindus.

There is a close relationship between the development and political participation of Sindhi Community because the Community is well aware of its participation in the politics. For the development of the Community as expected the development of the Community has taken place according to 53% of the people, but 31% of the people believe the development is not up to the mark expected.

It clearly indicates two meanings – The development took place due to politics and second meaning indicates that political activities must be undertaken for the development of the Community. The following table indicates all this. *(See Table No. 5:11)*

5:11 **Opinions about Political Participation of Sindhi Community regarding the development.**

No.	Relation between development and political participation	Quantity	Percentage
1.	Development as per expectation	53	53%
2.	Development not as per expectation	31	31%
3.	No Development at all	16	16%
	Total	**100**	**100%**

The Sindhi Community undertakes political moves for the financial development, which is must the Sindhi Community to cope up with the politics and it has that elasticity.

The following table is indicates this. *(See Table No. 5 : 12)*

5:12 **Type of adjustments with local community**

No.	Type of adjustments with local community	Quantity	Percentage
1.	To invite different political leaders and activists for programme	56	56%
2.	To offer share in financial institutions	00	00%
3.	Some other role	42	42%
4.	Not responded	02	02%
	Total	**100**	**100%**

The above table indicates, the Sindhi Community is a political community because this community doesn't allow the participation of ruling class in the Sindhi financial organizations. But it invites them for the other development of the community. This leads to support of other people to the Sindhi Community and they do not oppose the other community. They do believe in that the Sindhi Community is helpful to them and this leads to politics of consent.

The Sindhi Community is well aware of voting. 90% of the people in the community offer their valuable votes. This indicates their respect for democracy and support to democracy. Only 10% of them do not vote. The 90% of the voters are divided in two groups one of them advocates the political party and remaining group votes for as per directions of political leaders of the community. *(See Table No. 5 : 13)*

5:13   Voting method of Sindhi Community

Sr. No.	Types of voting	Quantity	Percentage
1.	Different political parties	56	56%
2.	As per directions of political leaders of the Community	34	34%
3.	No voting at all	10	10%
	Total	**100**	**100%**

Above table shows 56% of the Sindhi Community vote for different political parties and 34% of the people vote for the concern as per instructions given by the Sindhi leaders. This is clearly suggests that 34% of Sindhi Community favours imperative political culture. In short, imperative political participation is seen in Sindhi Community, where as 10% of the people are categorized under low political culture. The process of voting in politics definitely affects the politics and this is very well known to the Sindhi Community.

The get together programmes have been arranged for the political gains by the Sindhi Community. The nature of the programme is either religious, social or financial. If we assess the mediums and programmes for the political activation, one can conclude that religious, social and financial programmes are undertaken in the political framework. *(See Table No. 5:14)*

5:14   The mediums of Sindhi Community for the political Activation

Sr. No	Medium of political activation	Quantity	Percentage
1.	Religious programmes	28	28%
2.	Haldi Kunku / Samudaik Vivah (Collective Marriage Ceremony)	14	14%
3.	Felicitation of the students programmes	8	8%
4.	Felicitation programmes of the Community people	12	12%
5.	Banks, credit co-operative societies, Bhishi, women savings groups etc.	38	38%
	Total	**100**	**100%**

The above table shows 28% of the Sindhi Community people use religious programmes for the political activation of the Sindhi community. Where as 14% of the people arrange collective marriage ceremony programme to unite the women of the community together. Therefore, the concept of collective marriage ceremony become political.

To bring the youngsters together the felicitation of the students along with their collective marriage ceremony have been arranged by Sindhi Community, which relates the youngsters to the politics at an early stage. 12% of the people believe in the felicitation of the Sindhi Community people which connects the to political group. The last group is economical one. There is a close relationship between the Sindhi Community and the Financial organizations because 38% of the Sindhi Community people compels the political activation of the Sindhi Community through banks, credit co-operative societies, bhishi and women savings groups. This clearly shows the activation of politics of Sindhi Community work with social, religious and financial framework. It clearly indicates at the political activation level that the Sindhi Community is more practical than communalism and casteism.

Like the Hindus, the Sindhi Community also copes up with traditions and hence undertakes collective programmes. 91% of the Sindhi Community people do take part in the community programmes. In other words, to activate the Community people the religious programmes are undertaken. *(See Table No. 5:15)*

5:15   Opinions about celebrations of Religious programmes

Sr. No	Opinion about the religious programmes	Quantity	Percentage
1.	Participated in religious programmes	91	91%
2.	Not participated in religious programmes	06	06%
3.	Not responded	03	03%
	Total	**100**	**100%**

In brief, the Sindhi Community utilizes religious programmes for the political gains, because the above table shows that only 6% of the people does not participate in the religious programmes.

The Sindhi Community gives important to politics at local level. This community is also active on Maharashtra level, because decisions taken on this level directly affects their professions. The 10% of the people are active on the politics at national level. *(See Table No. 5:16)*

5:16   Levels of Political Participation of Sindhi Community

Sr. No	Levels of Political Participation of Sindhi Community	Quantity	Percentage
1.	Local	51	51%
2.	Maharashtra	25	25%
3.	India	10	10%
4.	All above levels	05	05%
5.	Not responded	09	09%
	Total	**100**	**100%**

According to the Sindhi Community the economic policy making must be decided by the Government of Maharashtra and Ahmednagar Municipal Corporation 58% of the people are of the opinion that Ahmednagar Municipal Corporation to stop the collecting octroi, where as 21% of the people believe that different factories should be started in Ahmednagar. At the same time 17% of Sindhi people are of the opinion that the Government should provide protection to traders. It means they believe that the Government should support trade from time to time and strengthen it. *(See Table No. 5:17)*

5:17 Opinions of Sindhi Community towards Government of Maharashtra and Ahmednagar Municipal Corporation

Sr. No.	Opinions of Sindhi Community	Quantity	Percentage
1.	To start different factories	21	21%
2.	To stop collecting of octroi	58	58%
3.	To start industries in compare with agriculture	02	02%
4.	To do investment in agriculture	02	02%
5.	To give security to trading	17	17%
	Total	**100**	**100%**

The special democratic values are deeply rooted in the Sindhi Community. In accordance with this attitude, the community people have enrolled their opinions regarding their right of voting 45% of the people believe the right of voting should be given to the literate people, where as 47% of them believe that, it should be universal. *(See Table No. 5:18)*

5:18   Attitude of Sindhi Community regarding the voting.

Sr. No.	Right of voting	Quantity	Percentage
1.	Literate	45	45%
2.	Illiterates	00	00%
3.	Women	08	08%
4.	Dalits	00	00%
5.	All above	47	47%
	Total	**100**	**100%**

Above table shows that, the people in Sindhi Community advocates the voting right in favour of literate and discards the illiterates. The Sindhi Community believes the literate people should be involved in political power. They believe that the voting right to all illiterates will not be of much use. It makes clear that the voting right to only literates makes democracy more mature. This Community also believe that power, authority and property should be controlled and governed by literates through voting. If most of the illiterate people are in power, the government will not be efficient and there will be no all sided development.

Which political party does the Sindhi Community votes for? this question was responded as follows. *(See Table No. 5 : 19)*

5:19 Classification of partywise voting of Sindhi Community

Sr. No.	Name of the party	Quantity	Percentage
1.	Congress	07	07%
2.	B.J.P.	28	28%
3.	Shivsena	34	34%
4.	N.C.P.	19	19%
5.	C.P.I.	01	01%
6.	Peasants Workers Party	00	00%
7.	M.N.S.	02	02%
8.	Not voted	02	02%
9.	As per the candidate	05	05%
10.	Not responded	02	02%
	Total	**100**	**100%**

The above table shows that 34% of the Sindhi Community people vote for the Shivsena and 28% believes in BJP. 19% of the people favour for N.C.P. and 7% of them to Congress Party. It indicates that the Sindhi Community favours the Shivsena and BJP than congress. They do believe more to Nationalist Congress Party than Congress. This is reason why Nationalist Congress Party has been elected in the Municipal Corporation Ulhasnagar. The corporators like Jyoti Kalani and other corporators of Sindhi Community are elected under the banner of N.C.P. This shows their attitude towards Nationalist Congress Party. Similarly the attitude of Sindhi Community of Ahmednagar seems towards N.C.P. Some Sindhi political leaders and traders expressed their opinion during the interview that former N.C.P. president of Ahmednagar District and Ex. MLA Dadabhau Kalamkar pays attention towards the progress of Sindhi Community. In 2015 nephew of N.C.P.

leader Dadabhau Kalamkar became the Mayor of Ahmednagar Corporation and it was noticed in survey that he gave priority to solve the problems of Sindhi colony which is near to his residence. *(See Table No. 5:20)*

5:20 The Participation of Sindhi youth in students' organizations

Sr. No.	Participation of Sindhi youth in students' organizations	Quantity	Percentage
1	Participation of Sindhi youth in Sindhi students' organizations	63	63
2	Participation of Sindhi youth in various political organizations	28	28
3	Participation of college going Sindhi youth in various organizations	09	09
	Total	**100**	**100**

It is the crucial level of political participation to be a part of various political and semi-political organizations along with our own caste. The ability for political participation is developed through it. The participation of Sindhi youth in the organizations established by Sindhi community is seen increasing . But the amount of young girls is very less in it. The amount of Sindhi young boys participating in various political parties in also seen increasing. Only 9 % of Sindhi youth has participated in various student's organizations in colleges. Most of the Sindhi youth seek admission to the commerce stream, attend 02 or 03 lectures and join the business started by their family. This is one of the reason for their less proportion of participation. *(See Table No. 5:21)*

5:21   The places of political discussions of Sindhi Community.

Sr. No.	Places of discussion	Quantity	Percentage
1	Family members and friends circle	04	04%
2	Elements in Community	06	06%
3	Credit Societies/ Bhishi Groups	18	18%
4	Religious Programmes	08	08%
5	Social Organizations	22	22%
6	Political Organizations	42	42%
	Total	**100**	**100%**

Where does the Sindhi Community discuss on the politics such a question was asked. According to answer given to the question, the most means upto 42% discussions are done on the political level. Next to it means 22% discussion is done at the levels of social organizations. Next to it, 18% people in Sindhi Community discuss about politics at the place and events of Credits Societies and Bhishi Groups. Only 4% of Sindhi Community is seen doing discussions about politics in the family. *(See Table No. 5:22)*

5:22 The participation of Sindhi traders in Organizations of traders

Sr. No.	The participation of Sindhi traders in their Organizations	Quantity	Percentage
1	The membership of various Trade-Associations (Retail trade Associations, Hoteliers Associations, Crackers Associations etc)	85	85%
2	Office Bearers of various trade Associations.	15	15%
	Total	**100**	**100%**

The trading associations is an important interest group. They are involved in unified attempts for fulfilling their demands. Sindhi traders, associations and Marwadi traders associations are viewed as important and major trade associations in the city. Retailers trade association, Hoteliers association, have members of Sindhi Community as their office bearers. From this information, it can be stated that Sindhi is a trading community. *(See Table No. 5:23)*

5:23 The participation of Sindhi Community in collection of funds for political parties

Sr. No.	Participation of Sindhi Community in collection of funds for political parties	Quantity	Percentage
1	Yes	72	72%
2	No	28	28%
	Total	**100**	**100%**

The political parties need funds for the canvass during elections as well as their usual programs. The leaders, party workers and well wishers of the political parties do the task of collecting funds for theirs parties. Mostly the political parties collect funds for elections of Municipal Corporation on large scale at local levels. Sindhi Community is at front in this case. After the coming of the funded party into power, the Sindhi Community tries to pressurise the party for formation of suitable economic policies. After the analysis of three elections of Ahmednagar Municipal Corporations, the party workers of BJP, Shivsena and NCP accepted that the Sindhi Community provided them the funds. *(See Table No. 5:24)*

5:24 The presence of Sindhi Community in meetings of political parties:

Sr. No.	The presence of Sindhi Community in meetings of political parties	Quantity	Percentage
1	Presence	84	84%
2	Absence	16	16%
	Total	**100**	**100%**

The political parties organize various meetings at the background of Lok Sabha, Vidhan Sabha and Municipal Corporation elections. Political parties play a major role as medium of political socialization. Political meetings reveal various issues at national, state and local level. 84% of Sindhi Community attends the meeting of various political parties. In result, the Sindhi Community is seen politically awaken on large scale. *(See Table No. 5:25)*

5:25   The Participation of Sindhi Community in various Agitations

Sr. No.	The Participation of Sindhi Community in various Agitations	Quantity	Percentage
1	The participation in agitation related to local issues (taxes of municipal corporation, for property taxes, the issues of depositors in close down credit societies, inefficiency of electricity board, the rape and murder case happened with a minor girl at Kopardi Village in Ahmednagar District etc.)	78	78%
2	The participation in the agitations related to state level issues (sales tax and other economic as well as business issues)	12	12%

3	The participation in the agitations related to national issues. (Movement by social worker Anna Hajare, Jan LokPal Bill, Anti Black money movement, the issue of religious conversions, etc.)	10	10%
	Total	**100**	**100%**

The Sindhi Community has participated in the various agitations related to political, social and economical issues. Therefore, the community is seen politically, socially and economically aware. 78% members of Sindhi Community are seen active in agitations related to local issues. Chiefly their participation was in the movements related to reduction of Octroi and property taxes, house tax, water tax etc. 12% of the Sindhi Community is seen involved in the agitations related to state level issues .In it, the stress is on the reduction of sales tax by the state government, reduction of economic restrictions on traders by the state government. The involvement of Sindhi Community in the agitations national important is very less. The Sindhi Community is seen less attentive to the issues like the movement of Anna Hajare at New Delhi, JanLokpal Bill, the issue of religious conversions in the country, etc.

The question regarding individual contribution for development of Sindhi Community was asked. It was responded as follows. *(See Table No. 5:26)*

5:26 Classification of the efforts for the development of Sindhi Community

Sr. No.	Type of contribution	Quantity	Percentage
1.	Financial Aid	08	08%
2.	Help for the students fees	06	06%
3.	Efforts for the employment	00	00%
4.	Efforts for gain loan to profession	07	07%
5.	Presentation of problems to the local ruling class	24	24%
6.	Social work for Sindhi community	34	34%
7.	Other answer	13	13%
8.	Not responded	08	08%
	Total	**100**	**100%**

Above table shows that 34% of the Sindhi Community people responded by saying that they do social work and hence, stress on to arrange collective marriages ceremonies, Diagnosis of all diseases arrange camps. 24% of the people are of the opinion that the difficulties of Sindhi Community are presented to the local ruling class. Only 7% of the people believe in the financial aids to the Sindhi Community but none of them believed to give employment.

6 | CONCLUSIONS

With reference to this study the following conclusions are arrived.

1. This research of Sindhi Community clearly shows that there is a political awareness in Sindhi Community. The impact of political economy, social, political and religious factors do effect on political socialization and political participation of the Sindhi Community.

2. The Sindhi Community is migrated. Hence, it compromised with the Hindu Community. The main reason for migration of Sindhi Community was Indo-Pak partition. Therefore, to oppose the Muslims was the abiding part of the politics of Sindhi Community. To oppose the Muslims was the enduring part of the Hindus too. Hence, this Sindhi Community and the Hindus united together on the issue of opposing Muslims. Their alliance on this is an important part of the political socialization of the Sindhi Community.

3. The Sindhi Community has tried to become majority group in the society. The Hindus are in majority. The Sindhi Community keeps contact with the Hindus. On the other hand, it is observed that less relations of Sindhi Community with Muslims, Christians and scheduled caste people. Therefore, we can interpret that the politics of Sindhi Community means politics of Hindus.

4. The Sindhi Community advocates capitalist economy and hence

accepts trading, industry and various types of services. And the classical and new classical liberal values belives the great effect on Sindhi Community. The attitudes of Sindhi Community are formed in the framework of these values. e.g. the Sindhi Community believes the Government of Maharashtra and Ahmednagar Municipal Corporation should increase the industry. Similarly the Community believe that Ahmednagar Municipal Corporation should stop the octroi. They also welcomed the innovative programs like 'Make In India' and 'Make In Maharashtra'. In short, Sindhi Community accepts the modernization in the framework of capitalism, and accepts the concept of democracy in the modern framework.

The political participation, political awareness and political socialization are the attitudes of Sindhi Community in the framework of the neo-classical liberalism. Therefore, this Sindhi Community instead of accepting the concept of social democracy accepts the elite democracy. The political socialization of the Sindhi Community had occurred due to attitude and values of elitism.

5. The Sindhi Community do politics for the financial gains and uses politics as a media for their development. Therefore, the financial gain is the object of Sindhi Community and politics is a mean. The Sindhi Community doesn't allow the ruling class to participate in its financial institutions, if means this community has a complete control on the financial institutions. 56% of the people cope up with their social activist and leaders, where as 42% of the Sindhi people believe in some other role. This clearly indicates two things

    a) The Sindhi Community does not allow politics in the economy but knew very well that the economy requires the protection of politics.

b) The Sindhi Community has the same direction regarding their political participation.

6. The Sindhi Community accepts the value based framework of the democracy, because this community respect democracy. 90% of the people from their community enjoy the right of voting and supports the democratic system. This means the Sindhi Community accepts the political participation in the framework of democracy.

7. The Sindhi Community does the collective type of politics. For the political activation they use various types of mediums like religious programmes, collective marriages, felicitation of students and meritorious community people, Banks, credit co-operative societies and women savings groups. The politics has to be done while living in this group. Therefore the programmes are to be arranged and the participation in groups is must. The Sindhi Community arranges get together programmes based on religion. These people participated in religious programmes and hence, the Sindhi Community is joined with the politics through religious programmes. In other words the attitude of this people towards politics is originated through religious programmes. Also through this programmes the political values and symbols have been accepted which shows that the political socialization of the Sindhi Community occurs through religious programmes.

8. The political participation of the Sindhi Community is seen on the local, state and national levels. It is the maximum on the local level, then it occurs on the state and lastly on the national level. Only 5% of them participates on all levels.

   The following figure shows the political participation of Sindhi Community of Ahmednagar City.

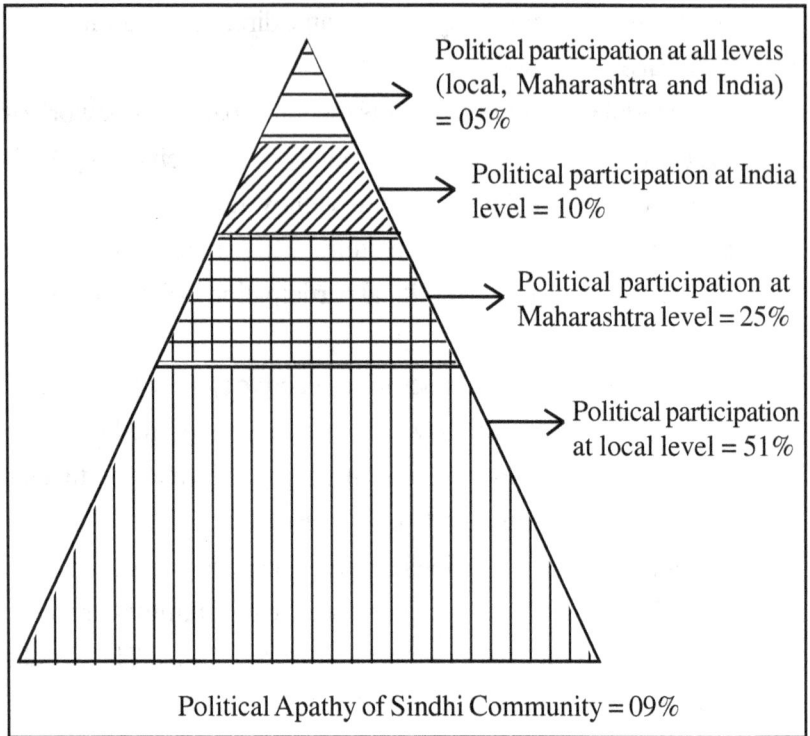

Political participation at all levels
(local, Maharashtra and India)
= 05%

Political participation at India
level = 10%

Political participation at
Maharashtra level = 25%

Political participation
at local level = 51%

Political Apathy of Sindhi Community = 09%

9. The Sindhi Community accepts the concept of literate peoples democracy. 45% of the people think that only the literate people should be given the right of voting. Most of them are not of the opinion that illiterate, dalits should not be given the right of voting. The attitude offering the right of voting to the literate people declares the Sindhi Community as having the elite attitude about the democracy. The conclusions regarding the democracy in this regards are as follows –

1. The Sindhi Community advocates that the political power should be in the hands of literate people.

2. Sindhi Community believes that in order to safeguard the interest of illiterates, the illiterates should not given more representation. They believe that if more illiterate people come in to power, it

will affect the industrial progress of the country and thereby hinder their progress in trade and industry.

3.   The Sindhi Community did not seen in favor of participation at women in politics. But the community insists on the voting right to women.

According to Sindhi Community the concept of political power is of specialists. In the concept of power the Sindhi Community has literate people at the center and the remaining factors are on the circumference.

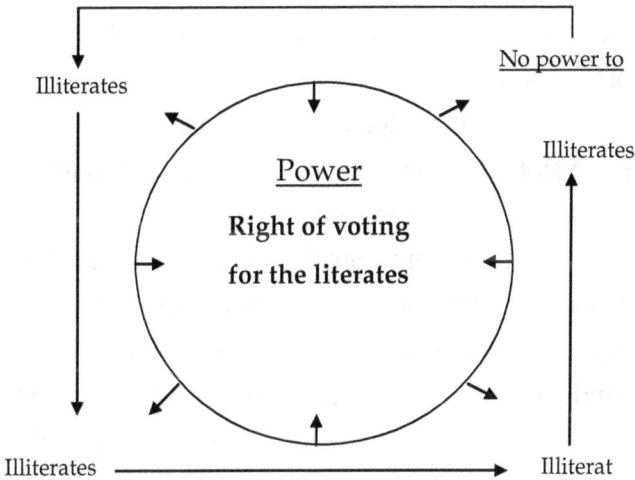

10.   The Sindhi Community does politics for the economical development. The question, whether the Sindhi Community does politics for the welfare of the Mahrashtrians as well as the Indians, is not answered. The 34% of people do social type of works for the development of the community. The Sindhi Community helps to solve 24% of the problems with help of local ruling class. In short, the development of the Sindhi Community is the core of politics and it is assumed by the Sindhi Community and hence the participation politics occurs in it.

11. The Sindhi Community undertakes various kinds of professions. This community is concentrated in the various fields like shopkeeping, industries and service sectors, so it is of a practical mind. Therefore, the participation in politics does have this practical out look. As a result the political sphere is not chosen as a fulltime said work, and hence professions have been executed successfully. The politics is used for the protection of the professions. In other words the Sindhi Community does not accepts the concept of autonomy of political power. The Sindhi Community does not believed the political power as goal by opting the political powers. On the contrary, they believe the existence of their professions based on politics. Therefore, it is the political awareness of Sindhi Community the political power should protect professions, law and order should be maintained and for the better execution of the professions law and order is must. This Sindhi Community does not completely depend upon political power. Their existence is in the financial powers. They believe in the politics for the dominance of financial powers. Therefore the Sindhi Community develops the political awareness for the protection of financial relations and believes the Legislature, Executive, Judiciary and Local Governments as means, and not objects. So the politics of Sindhi Community itself is at the centre of development.

12. It is observed that the Sindhi Community is politically matured. It has its high political participation and reason for this is that the Sindhi Community is literate and having literacy in various fields. 32% of the people in this Sindhi Community are Graduates 11% of them have completed their Post Graduation. The professional education has been obtained by 7%, 28% of them have completed their secondary and higher secondary education. In short, this

community is educated and based on values of literate presently. Their attitudes are based on literacy and practical outlets. Therefore, it is observed that their politics based on financial gains and their political participation is not impracticable. This is the speciality of the political participation of this community.

The Sindhi Community is of the opinion that the politics should occur in the framework of elitism or expertise democracy. The power should be in the hands of expert people like professionals. Therefore, the Sindhi Community advocates changed world level economy after 1991 and free economic policy of the country. Hence, the Sindhi Community believes that there should be co-ordination between the international market and the local market, and such type of freedom should be given by state. It is the contemporary political awareness of Sindhi Community that the state government should pay sufficient attention to the law and order in the state.

13.   The behavior of the Sindhi Community in Ahmednagar is based on the religious framework. And even their political and economical framework matches to this. The Sindhi Community arranges religious programes and through them recycles the Hindu traditions. These sentiments have been carried out in politics too. This means the Sindhi Community in Ahmednagar city has a cult for Shivsena and BJP. This research shows that 34% and 28% of the Sindhi Community people voted for Shivsena and BJP respectively. The percentage of these two equal to 62%. 19% of them voted for N.C.P. , 7% of them for Congress and 2% to MNS. The Communist Party was voted by 1% Sindhi people. This clearly indicates the cult of Sindhi Community towards Shivsena and Bhartiya Janta Party.

After BJP and Shivsena the cult of Sindhi Community seemed to NCP. It is because their prolonged power in Ulhasnagar Municipal Corporation. That is why the cult of Sindhi Community seemed towards NCP than Congress. It was found that there was an active group who accept the leadership of Sharad Pawar. In Vidhan Sabha election of 2014, for the first time MLA of NCP was elected in Ahmednagar city. Similarly in 2015, nepnew of NCP former President of Ahmednagar District and Ex. MLA Dadabhau Kalamkar became the Mayor of Ahmednagar Municipal Corporation and he gave priority to solve the problems of Sindhi Community.

BIBLIOGRAPHY

- Ahmednagar District Gazetteers, 1976, Gazetteers Department, Bombay.
- Advani Behrumal Maharchand, 1990, History of Hindus in Sindh, Sharada Publishers, Mumbai.
- Advani L. K., 2008, My Country My Life, Rupa and Co., New Delhi.
- Ahmednagar Municipal Corporation, Budget 2012-2013, Ahmednagar.
- Anand Subhadra, 1996, National Integration of Sindhis, Vikas Publications, New Delhi.
- Census of India, Maharashtra Population Data, 2011.
- Dowse S.E. and Hughes J. A.; 1972, Political Sociology, John Willey and Sons, London.
- Das Hari Hara, 1998, Political system of India, Amol Publications, New Delhi.
- District Statistical Office, Ahmednagar, Economical and Social Evaluation, 2014-15.
- Hardwani Lachman, 1992, Marathi – Sindhi Lexicon, Maharashtra Rajya Sahitya Sanskruti Mandal, Mumbai.
- Hardwani Lachman;, 1995 Sindhi–Marathi Lexicon (Devnagari Script) Ahmednagar.
- Hiranandani, Popati; 1980, Sindhis: The Scattered Treasure, Malaah Publications, New Delhi.

- Inamdar N.R., 1972, Community Development and Democracy Growth, Popular, Mumbai.

- Inamdar and Puranik, 1984, Rajkiya Samajshastra (Marahti), Continental, Pune.

- Inamdar and Vakil, Modern Political Analysis (Marathi), 1984, Shubhada Saraswat Publishers, Pune.

- Johari J. C., Comparative Politics, 1998, Sterling, New Delhi.

- Kamble Bal, 2003, Unpublished UGC Minor Research Project entitled- 'Political, Social, Economical profile of a Community : A study of Marwadi Community in Ahmednagar City..

- Kamble Bal, Election of Ahmednagar Municipal Corporation – 2003, 'Political Economy of Ahmednagar City' published article in newspaper on 17th and 18th March 2004.

- Kaushik Shushila, 1993, Women's Participation in Politics, Vikas publishers, New Delhi.

- Kochanek Stanley A , 1974, Business and Politics in India, University California Press, Berkerly, Landon (U.K.)

- Lele Jayant;, 1982 Elite Pluralism and Class Rule : Political Development in Maharashtra, Popular, Mumbai.

- Lohiya Ram Manohar, India - Pak partition (Marathi) Lokmangmaya Granth, Mumbai.

- Malkani K. R., 1987, The Sindh Story, Allied Publications Pvt Ltd, Sindhi Academy. Delhi.

- Marathi Vishwakosh, 1976, Volume I, Maharashtra Rajya Marathi Vishwakosh Nirmiti Mandal.

- Mirikar N. Y. (Sardar), 2016, Ahmednagar Shahracha Etihas, Ahmednagar Historical Musium, Ahmednagar.

- Mukhi H. R., 1997, Political Sociology, SBD Publishers, New Delhi.

- Nagrikshstra and Prashashan Kosh (Marathi), 2001, Maharashtra

State Bureau of Textbook Production and Curriculum Research, (Balbharti) Pune.

- Palshikar Suhas, Birmal Nitin, Pawar Prakash (Ed.) 2004, Maharashtrache Rajkaran – Rajkiya Prakriyeche Stanik Sandharbha (Marahti), Pratima Prakashan, Pune.
- Pavlov V.I, 1964, The Indian Capitalist Class, New Delhi.
- Urvashi Butalla, The Sindhi Identity, Book Review of Rita Kothari's 'The Burden of Refugee : The Sindhi Hindus of Gujrat,' Economical and Political Weekly, May 5, 2007.
- Rush and Altoff, 1972, An Introduction to Political Sociology, Nelson's University Paper Bracks, Great Britain.
- Sharma Shankuntala, 1994, Grassroots Politics and Panchayati Raj, Deep and deep Publishers, New Delhi.
- 'Sindhi People' (undated) Wikipedia website (http://en.wikipedia.org/wiki/Sindhi_People).
- Sindhis in India (from Wikipedia, the free encyclopedia).
- Sindhis Spread All over India, 2008, Collected Research Data by Sindhi Consolidation Center.
- Sirsikar V.M., 1965, Political Behaviour in India, Pune.
- Sudhakar V., 2002, New Panchayat Raj System, Local Self Government in Community Development, Mangaldeep Publications, New Delhi.
- Samaj Vidnyan Kosh (Marathi), Volume – II
- Sindhi Pariwarik Nirdeshika – 2003 (Marahti), Prepared by Shrichand Talrejea on behalf of Swami Tahuram Mandir Trust, Ahmednagar.
- Thakur U. T., 1997, Sindhi Culture , Sindhi Academy, Delhi.
- Vora Rajendra and Palshikar Suhas, 1987, Rajyashastra Kosh (Marathi), Dastane and Co., Pune.

- Website : www. eci.govt.in
- Website : www. yashada.in

Newspapers :
1. Dainik Hindu. (in Sindhi and Arabic script - Mumbai and Ahmedabad)
2. Leader Express. (Ulhasnagar)

Weekly :
1. Hindwasi, (Mumbai)
2. Maharal, (Ulhasnagar)
3. Sindhi Report, (Ahmedabad)

Fortnightly :
1. Dil – E – Hind, Fortnightly Samachar Patra (New Delhi)

Trimonthly :
1. Kunj (Mumbai)
2. Shudha Sahittik, (Mumbai)
3. Simpoo (Mumbai)
4. Rachana (Adipur – Gujrat)

Magazines :
Akhand Sindhu Sansar - Devnagari Script (Bhopal)

Sindhi Classical Literature :
1. Sachal Jo Kalam (Sachal Sarmasta)
2. Shah Jo Rasolo (Shah Abdul Latiff)
3. Samia Ja Salok (Samee)

About the Author

Dr. Bal Kamble

Author Dr. Bal Kamble is an eminent scholar in the subject of Political Science. He has 30 years of teaching experience and right now he is serving as a Principal at Rayat Shikshan Sanstha's Dada Patil Mahavidyalaya, Karjat in Ahmednagar district. Throughout his career he has been actively engaging himself in political, economical, social research and service of the education.

Dr. Kamble has participated in many national and international level seminars and conferences. He has published various articles and books on Political Theory, Political Process, Public Administration and Competitive Examinations. Along with these activities, he has completed various research projects funded by UGC and BCUD, SPPU, Pune. He is selected as the Sammelanadhyaksha of 34th Maharashtra Political Science and Public Administration Parishad.

www.ingramcontent.com/pod-product-compliance
Lightning Source LLC
Chambersburg PA
CBHW050555280326
41933CB00011B/1849

9788184836967